# MUSICAL WOMEN
# THROUGHOUT HISTORY

---

## THE WOMEN WHO FOUGHT FOR MUSIC

## CHRISTINE BENNET

# NO PLACE FOR A WOMAN SERIES

Adventurous Women Throughout History:
Women In History That Other Women Should Read About

Royal Women Throughout History:
Biographies About Royal Women From All Different Countries
Through The Ages

Musical Women Throughout History:
The Women Who Fought For Music

Smart Women Throughout History:
Intelligent Women Who Had Great Ideas

Heroic Women Throughout History:
The Women Who Didn't Back Down Because It Got Too Hard

More Musical Women Throughout History:
More Women Who Fought For Music

# MUSICAL WOMEN THROUGHOUT HISTORY

## THE WOMEN WHO FOUGHT FOR MUSIC

## CHRISTINE BENNET

*For all the women out there who forged ahead*
*with their musical careers,*
*Thank You*

# CONTENTS

Christine Bennet

# INTRODUCTION

When looking for inspiration on how to lead a happy and successful life, the best place to start is by examining the lives of the women who came before us. These women have left a blueprint for us to follow, and we can use their knowledge and power to overcome adversities in our own lives. So many women have led amazing and fascinating lives. They exhibited endurance, talent, and bravery during some of the toughest periods of history. I believe that no matter what you are going through, you can always find strength in learning about these women and how they handled their own challenges.

The tales of these women can bolster your confidence and ability to just keep going. As women, we have a remarkable capacity for perseverance, and we are so resilient. I know that you have already overcome so many challenges in your life with strength and boldness. Well, *Musical Women Throughout History* aims to keep you on track with interesting stories and fascinating tidbits about the women who came before you. I know that you will be able to find parallels in your own life and relate to some of the struggles that these women experienced.

Creativity is one of the most important attributes a woman can possess. It helps us open our minds to new possibilities and ways of handling big life emotions and changes. Creativity boosts problem-solving skills and decision-making. In this book, I will focus on women who harnessed the power of music to make meaningful changes in the world. There are so many stories about strong women in the music industry, and, of course, there is no way to cover them all! On that note, I've selected a handful of the most captivating stories to share with you. The women in these pages shaped so many different aspects of music, from classical to blues to rock. Without them, the world wouldn't be the same.

In my experience, learning about women in history has really helped me progress through my own personal life. I find that their stories are so inspirational that they further my own resilience. If they could do it, so can I! Many of their challenges ring true to my life, and I find the tidbits about who they were as people to be the most interesting part of their stories. They help me relate to their lives and what they went through. You'll see, as you read along, that their lives and personalities bear a resemblance to yours. It's endlessly fascinating how times can change, yet the struggles of women—and their ability to overcome challenges —are still relatable to us modern women.

In this book, you will find stories about people such as Hildegard von Bingen, a woman who lived in the 1100s and founded two monasteries while also being a prolific composer. There is also Louise Farrenc, who demanded to receive equal pay as her male contemporaries. Ethel Smyth was a woman who lived a long life and is considered one of the most influential and accomplished composers of all time. Opera singer Nellie Melba has been immortalized on the $100 note in Australia. You'll also learn the story of Bessie Smith, known as "the Empress of Blues." I will then explore the life of Billie Holiday and her contribution to jazz music, as well as her friend and rival, Ella Fitzgerald. You'll read about the fascinating tale of country icon Patsy Cline, along with powerhouse Aretha Franklin. From there, we will explore the sad story of psychedelic soul singer Janis Joplin, as well as the tragic life of the immensely gifted Karen Carpenter. Finally, I will finish the book off with the Aussie icon Chrissy Amphlett and a look into her massive role in changing rock music

All of these women paved the way for future female musicians. They changed the course of history and are remembered for their contributions and tenacity. Without them, we wouldn't be where we are today. Modern music stars like Adele and Taylor Swift have these women to thank for all their success. Indeed, female artists are now considered equal to and in some cases better than males in the same industry. While there is always a long way to go for women around the world to achieve new heights and overdue respect, we have come a long way—in large part to the women in this very book.

So, if you are looking for a boost in confidence and a deeper sense of inner strength, join me as I explore these amazing women and their stories.

# 1

## HILDEGARD VON BINGEN (1098-1179)

Hildegard von Bingen is considered by many to have changed the face of classical music. Besides acknowledging that right off the bat, her talents and contributions to the world do not stop there. She was an incredibly intelligent woman who famously cataloged the flora and fauna of her native German Rhineland and developed medical theories that are still practiced in holistic therapy to this day (BBC Music Magazine, 2019). She was a woman deeply connected to her religious beliefs, experiencing visions sent from God throughout her life. This devotion has been recognized in significant ways, leading right up till today: Perhaps most notably, in 2012, Pope Benedict XVI recognized Hildegard as a saint (Martin, 2012). This sainthood was appointed due to her invaluable contribution to the Catholic Church. She spread the word of God throughout her life and provided a renewed spirituality for many people in the 12th century. Not only was she a spokesperson for her religion, she also wrote works of theology, including poems, all the while composing music that has stood the test of time.

As you can imagine, being a woman in the Middle Ages wasn't easy. In Hildegard's time, it wasn't particularly common for women to write and perform music. Medieval women were almost entirely dependent on the men in their lives. They weren't able to own property, sign contracts, or have money under their control. Most commonly, they needed to be married and rely on their husbands for their livelihood. While medieval women could work, performing tasks such as tailoring and cooking, their money would go to their husbands. As Hildegard was a nun, she was able to overstep this societal standard, instead relying deeply on the Church to provide her with basic needs.

Hildegard's talents have at times been overshadowed by her male contemporaries. Nowadays, her contributions to the art of composing are celebrated. Her choice of instrument was the 10-stringed psaltery, which resembles a modern-day harp. She also wrote music that was intended to be sung out loud by a solitary performer.

Hildegard's story is one of a late bloomer. Indeed, she didn't start composing music until she was in her 40s. She's an early example of successfully changing careers, even as you get older. I know for modern women, this challenge is ever present. We often believe that once we have chosen a career path, we must stick it out. Through Hildegard's story, we can take inspiration and know that this isn't true at all; you can pursue your passions at any age. There is no need to put yourself in a box. While this change in her life direction wasn't an easy one, she persevered and ended up in the history books for her talents. She portrayed confidence in a time when women were expected to be meek and submissive and refused to be silenced by the societal expectations of 12th century Germany.

Hildegard's life story is brimming with accolades and achievements. She made countless contributions to so many different facets of life. She believed that, regardless of her station as a middle-aged nun, she could do more than one thing in her life, and so she took up challenges with gusto. In short, Hildegard von Bingen is proof that women are capable of excelling at more than one thing. Our talents are endless. We just need to find the strength to explore them.

## A Brief History

Hildegard von Bingen was born in 1098 in Alzey, a region of Rheinhessen in Germany. This part of the country was (and still is) one of the biggest wine regions in the country. Her family fell into the class of lower nobility. Her parents, Mechtild of Merxheim-Nahet and Hildebert of Bermersheim, owned some land, although they were not particularly rich or prominent members of society. Hildegard is thought to be the 10th child of approximately 14 children in total. That's right—there are clear records of her having at least seven older siblings!

Hildegard was a sickly child. She began experiencing visions at roughly three years of age. These caused her debilitating headaches, meaning that she wasn't able to help the family earn money, as was expected of children in this era. Due to her ailments, her family made the decision to give her away to a Benedictine abbey. This wasn't uncommon; giving away children to the Church was a way for many families to pay taxes.

Once at the abbey, Hildegard became an anchoress. According to Dr. Mary Wellesley, "an anchoress was a woman who was walled into a cell to live a life of prayer and contemplation" (Wellesley, 2018). Hildegard was unable to leave her cell for any reason. The theory was that those in anchorage would die and then rise to a position of immortality due to their devotion. She lived in this way for more than three decades of her life, having only one companion during this time, a high-born girl named Countess Jutta von Sponheim. The two young women prayed and meditated together every day. They learned scriptures, and it is theorized that it was during this time that Hildegard learned how to play the 10-stringed psaltery. Jutta was able to teach Hildegard basic Latin, as well as a little bit about the outside world. This served as Hildegard's only form of education.

Once Jutta passed away in 1136, Hildegard was released from her cell. Hildegard was to become a prioress, which is a type of nun. In this role, she would be under the authority of Abbot Kuno of Disibodenberg. Hildegard was unhappy with this and wanted independence, so she appealed to the archbishop to allow her to move to a temporary dwelling. As a result, she was moved to a monastery in 1150 and was even considered a founder of this monastery, as she was integral to its formation. Later on, in 1165, Hildegard formed a second monastery for n uns.

## VISIONS

The visions Hildegard had are a huge part of her story. She claimed that God would send her messages through all five of her senses. This contributed to her success as a nun and is likely the reason she was able to open her own monasteries. She was seen as being deeply in touch with

God, and thus a vessel for his word. These visions took an enormous toll on her health, however. As I previously mentioned, they would give her splitting headaches that would result in her being bedridden for long periods of time.

Hildegard's first foray into music was, in fact, a direct result of her visions. A message from God told her to "write down that which you see and hear" (Ruether, 2002). While the visions caused her great pain, she began to write about the messages she was receiving. This led to Pope Eugenius developing an interest in Hildegard, as he was intrigued by her writing.

### Visionary Works

In her lifetime, Hildegard wrote three important pieces of visionary theology. These included musical compositions, poetry, and nearly 400 letters. She published her first major composition entitled *Scivias* between 1142 and 1151. Unfortunately, though preserved for centuries afterward, this piece of writing was lost in the 1940s. She was in her 40s at the time writing *Scivias*, and would go on to write a composition entitled *Liber Vitae Meritorum*, between 1158 and 1163. Additionally, she wrote *Liber Divinorum Operum* in 1163.

## HILDEGARD AND MUSIC

Her visionary compositions gained great popularity in the medieval Catholic Church. In total, Hildegard wrote approximately 60–80 compositions. These were all original pieces of work, some written in poetic form, others as liturgical songs. She wrote hymns that were sung in churches across the country and became an integral part of religious services.

As influential as she was in her own time, Hildegard's music paved the way for modern music as well. Many of today's popular hymns are based on her original work. She has reportedly influenced many other composers, and some writers have used her text as a basis for their own pieces of work.

What is incredibly impressive about Hildegard is that she had no musical training. She was self-taught and practiced the art of the 10-stringed psaltery throughout her life to further her abilities. Even with limited education, she was able to write eloquently about the visions she was receiving from God and was highly respected for her talents.

To understand what Hildegard's music sounded like, I'll ask you to imagine it as being similar to rhythmic chanting. She would move up and down in octaves while chanting her lyrics, creating the basis of how hymn music sounds in the contemporary age. Again, she is primarily credited for the development of modern day hymns, with some of her lyrics even being borrowed to create new songs.

In her songwriting, Hildegard rebelled against the normal sound of music at the time. She would experiment with different styles and improvise sounds to develop a new and uniquely formed presentation of music to the public. Indeed—she would freely take liberties with the existing sounds of her time to create something even better.

In 1994, a record label called Angel released a CD based on Hildegard's music entitled *Vision: The Music of Hildegard von Bingen* (Johnson, 2019). Versions of her music are also available on YouTube.

## HEALING AND MEDICINE

Hildegard wasn't just going to stop at music. She utilized the power of her visions to develop pieces of work devoted to healing and connecting to the physical world. Additionally, she harnessed her own experience with medical issues and her time as an anchoress to develop ideas about spiritual healing. In doing so, she became known as a healer herself. Her passion for researching and experimenting with alternative methods made her popular in her community, and people traveled to see her in hopes that she would be able to assist them with their ailments.

Her piece *Physica* outlines how plants, gemstones, and animals could be used in connection to healing the human body (Colby, 2019). This is considered to be the first text that explores the use of brewed hops as a preservative (Kitsock, 2014). It is estimated that she wrote this between 1150 and 1158. Keep in mind that this was also while she was writing some of the most influential pieces of music of the Middle Ages. Suffice it to say, she certainly kept busy in the latter half of her life.

She still wasn't done: Hildegard also wrote *Causae et Curae*, which delved into the topic of personal health. The date when she published this work is seemingly lost to history. In this book, she developed theories about what diets would be best depending on the season. As well, she connected nature to different diseases and concocted various home remedies for common ailments. She believed that by examining a person's gender, menstrual cycle, veins, and stool, one could provide clues on what they were suffering from. This included advice on how to treat fractures, dislocations, and burns. Hildegard used this text to connect spirituality to health. She suggested that there needed to be a balance of elements within a person's being (Sweet, 1999).

Holistic practitioners and spiritual healers still use Hildegard's theories as a basis for treatment. She was right on the money for several of her cures and ideas, and made an impactful contribution to how people are treated centuries after her death.

## HILDEGARD'S LEGACY

Honey Meconi, a professor of music at the Eastman School of Music and University of Rochester, has worked for many years to compile the story of Hildegard von Bingen. When she reflects on Hildegard's personality, she says:

> Hildegard was also someone who didn't accept her place in the world. She wrote her books, and created a new language, and, in a male-dominated church, she went on preaching tours at a time when women were not supposed to preach, especially in public. She refused to behave in a certain way. She wrote at a time when, if the church authorities had not thought she was divinely inspired, she could easily have been put to death as a heretic (Colby, 2019).

Hildegard was a tenacious woman in a time when this quality could have been the reason for her death. She actively worked against the status quo and didn't allow her gender to limit her ability to make a change in the world. She is remembered for her compositions and contributions to hymns and religious music. Her ability to promote the Church earned her sainthood, and her medical theories are still in practice today.

The story of Hildegard von Bingen's life is a reminder that we are all multifaceted people. Even when our young lives are difficult—say, we are put in a cell and not allowed to leave it for 30 years—we can still persevere and make something of ourselves. Hildegard serves as an inspiration to try out new things, no matter our age. She was confident that she would succeed in anything she put her mind to and proved any naysayers wrong. If a woman in the Middle Ages could make this much change and contribute to modern society with so much influence, there is no reason that any of us can't follow in her footsteps and do the same.

.

# 2

---◆◇◆---

# LOUISE FARRENC (1804-1875)

The Romantic period in music would not be the same without the contributions of the amazing Louise Farrenc. Louise was a French composer, world-renowned pianist, and teacher of music. She was so talented that she became a professor at the famous Paris Conservatory, where she was once a student. She had a deep love for composition and wrote pieces that have endured into the modern era. While her passion was always directed at the piano, she also experimented with the violin and other string instruments. Louise was not only a powerhouse musician, though: She was also an incredibly strong woman. She is remembered for her fight for equality and resilience during a time when women were not considered as talented or intelligent as men.

Louise was born in the aftermath of the French Revolution. In the 1800s, women were expected to stay out of the public sphere and essentially live their lives in the shadows of men. They were burdened with all the domestic duties and were reliant on their husbands and male counterparts for their basic needs. However, the Revolution sparked newfound ideas in French women. They began expressing their thoughts on politics and their frustrations with how the country was being run. Upper-class women began to fight for the right to own property and suffrage, while working-class women began taking to the streets to protest the rising cost of basic needs, like a loaf of bread (Spiegel, 2020). This is considered by some historians to be the first wave of feminism in France. Women's unions were secretly started, with the objective of fighting for equal pay, the right to divorce, and education for girls. Still, this period of time is referred to as the "cult of domesticity" (Goldstein, 2020). Despite a shift toward modernity, women were still expected to remain in their "rightful" place, standing by their husbands and families. French suffragettes wouldn't have a platform until 1909.

The subsequent waves of feminism that would come in the years following Louise's death are, in part, a reflection of her own stance against inequality. She was one of the first women to speak out publicly against unfair pay standards and leveraged her great talent to be heard by influential men.

The name Louise Farrenc has been somewhat forgotten with time. In the Romantic era, there were dozens of notable male composers and pianists making names for themselves, and with the competitive nature of longevity, Louise's contributions have often been overshadowed by those of her male contemporaries. Of course, I strongly believe that her story is one that every person should know—and relish the opportunity to share it here. She was greatly influential, and her musical flair was unmatched. Beyond her talent, though, Louise is also someone to reflect on solely for the reason that we should always remember the women who fought for our rights, especially when it was dangerous for them to do so. Louise was not one to back down or give up. She's proof that if you stand for something, you need to speak loudly and proudly about your beliefs.

Louise's influence on music and feminism is fascinating. I see so many parallels between her life and the lives lived by many modern women. So many of us work in industries that are dominated by males, and even when we are more talented than them, we can still be overlooked. It can be easy to become disheartened when you feel like you'll never get a break due to your gender, and when I feel this way myself, I look to women like Louise Farrenc for inspiration. Her perseverance reminds me that I have the strength within me to keep going as well. She used her voice to ignite a movement, and we can all do the same.

# A BRIEF HISTORY

Louise was born Jeanne-Louise Dumont on the 31st of May, 1804, in Paris. Her father, Jacques-Edme Dumont, was an incredibly successful sculptor who famously won The Prix de Rome, a highly sought-after scholarship. This wasn't her only famous relative, though. Her brother, Augustin-Alexandre Dumont, was also a famous sculptor who was awarded the same scholarship as his father and went on to become a teacher at an exclusive art school in France. Needless to say, Louise grew up around artists and visionaries. Her young life was infused with creative flair. Her family was considered to be quite bohemian, and she was exposed to the wisdom and ways of artistic women in a manner that many girls her age were not. This exposure in her formative years undoubtedly influenced her perception of the world. She understood that women could be just as artistic as men. Furthermore, women didn't have to be bound to domestic duties; they could do so much more.

By all accounts, Louise showed musical talent from a young age. She began practicing the piano as soon as she could and was immediately recognized by the greats of her time as someone to keep an eye on. Some of these greats included Johann Nepomuk Hummel and Ignaz Moscheles, both of whom are remembered as virtuoso pianists. They gave Louise lessons and guidance, building her up to become a child protege. Louise also started to show an aptitude for composing her own music. She experimented with her creativity, laying the foundation for her future success.

In 1819, Louise's parents decided to send her to study composition at the Paris Conservatoire. She was just 15. She began to take private lessons at the school, although she was not allowed to perform in public or to join classes with other pupils. In fact, the school remained publically closed to women until 1870 (Duchen, 2021). To be clear, females were allowed to attend, although only in private. She primarily took lessons with Anton Reicha, who is best known for his contribution to quintet literature. Interestingly, he was also a good friend of Beethoven's, and they reportedly composed music together. All this is to say that Louise was constantly surrounded by very influential men in the music industry of the 19th century. While the male students were given the opportunity to perform and shine, and thus grow their popularity and audience, Louise's flourishing talents remained in the dark. Still, she didn't allow this treatment to stop her from pursuing her passion. Her family was very supportive of her dream of being a pianist and encouraged her to keep going.

### Louise and Aristide

Louise married early in life, like many women of her era. At 17, she wed Aristide Farrenc, who was 10 years her senior. Aristide was a flute player. There are two tales about how the pair met: First, Aristide regularly performed at the artist's colony of the Sorbonne. Louise's family frequently visited the Sorbonne, and their courtship could have started there. Another theory is that the two met at the conservatory, where they were both students. Reportedly, the two were good friends, and this was a happy union.

After they married, Louise paused her studies to travel with her husband across France. Together, they would perform music at various venues. It was Louise's first real taste of playing for an audience. Unfortunately, Aristide lost interest in performing after a few years and wanted to settle down. The pair started a publishing house called *Éditions Farrenc*. This publishing house was unbelievably popular in France. It became one of the leading music publishers in the country for 40 years.

Back in Paris, Louise resumed her studies with Anton Reicha. In 1826, at age 22, she paused her lessons again for the birth of her daughter, Victorine. As Victorine grew, she also proved to be an amazing concert pianist. She performed just as her mother had, until she sadly passed away at the early age of 32.

## LOUISE AND MUSIC

When Louise returned to music for the third time, she started composing some of the highest quality concert pieces, which notably demanded extreme skill from anyone looking to perform them (Duchen, 2021). Her music may never have gained popularity if not for the publishing house and its success. Aristide was extremely passionate about encouraging his wife. In 1838, they published a substantial piece of her work under the name *Trente études dans tous les tons majeurs et mineurs* (Duchen, 2021).

By 1845, this became a compulsory piece of study for all piano students at the Paris Conservatoire.

Breaking a long-standing tradition, Louise became the second female piano professor to teach at the conservatory in 1842. A female hadn't taught there since the previous century. Up until she was appointed professor, she had worked tirelessly at composing and performing. And her hard work didn't stop there—her sights were set on promoting female pianists and encouraging girls to take up the art. All her students were female, and a large number went on to find great successes of their own. Many of them went on to win the Premier Prix at the institution, meaning, too, that they graduated with the highest honor. This is astounding, considering it would still be a few decades until the school opened its doors to female students to perform publicly and take lessons alongside male students. Louise was poetic in her style, encouraging creativity and experimentation. For her, the piano wasn't a rigid instrument that could only be played one way—indeed, she saw endless possibilities for herself and for her students. She held her position at the conservatory for 30 years.

Louise never stopped writing. No matter how busy she was with teaching and motherhood, composition was always at the forefront of her mind. She expanded her talent. Rather than just writing compositions for the piano, she began composing for orchestras and symphonies as well. Researchers note that this was not typical of women at this time (Duchen, 2021). It's clear to see that she was breaking barriers in the musical world in any way that she could.

Louise was also unique in her style. It was popular at the time to write opera pieces, although she was more interested in experimenting with sonatas and symphonies. One could interpret Louise as someone who had no interest in becoming famous. If she did, she likely would have conformed and tried her hand at writing an opera. Yet, she was more interested in teaching and expressing herself through music. Perhaps her legacy would be more pronounced if she had conformed, that just wasn't Louise's goal. Her personality was that of a free spirit and creator. She wanted to inspire passion and creativity. She reminds us that we don't have to do things the same way as others just to fit in. To truly be happy, we need to follow our hearts and do what gives us joy.

When tragedy struck the family in the form of Victorine's death in 1859, Louise stopped composing altogether. She continued teaching, however, and assisted Aristide with his passion for researching music. They created a multi-anthology work after compiling research on centuries of musical history. In this way, the pair contributed to musical evolution, with one writer noting, "When, in the wake of the Franco-Prussian War, a new generation of composers set about reinventing French style by exploring the Baroque harpsichordists, somebody had already done the groundwork" (Duchen, 2021).

## *Symphony No. 3*

One of Louise Farrenc's best-known works is her 1847 piece "Symphony No. 3." It is said that this piece was influenced by Beethoven through Anton Reicha's teaching. Nina Green of *BBC Music Magazine* describes the piece as "plentiful, particularly in the final movement, which opens with bold and ample strings. The Adagio movement is equally glorious, transforming from a gentle clarinet and oboe melody to full-bodied symphonic pleasure very early on" (Green, 2019). The piece has a clarity of structure and thought and creates powerful momentum. It has since been famously performed by Johannes Goritzki, the North German Radio Philharmonic Orchestra, Stefan Sanderling, and the Orchestre de Bretagne (Service, 2014). You can purchase a recording of these performances or find them on YouTube.

## *Violin Sonata in A*

Louise's legacy in music isn't just confined to her extraordinary skills as a pianist. She is also remembered for her composition of "Violin Sonata in A" in 1850. There are four violin movements in this piece, all of them incredibly varied in sound and still coming together to make a magical piece of music. Some musicians believe that they can hear a hint of Mozart toward the end of the first movement. This piece is so popular that you can find several different renditions on music streaming services.

## *Nonet*

Louise's 1849 composition "Nonet" is considered to be her most popular piece. Written for a combination of a string quartet and a wind quintet, she deviated from the piano once again to write an exemplary piece of music. During her lifetime, this was Louise's closest brush with fame. It led to her rising popularity across the European continent, with performers entranced by her unique sound and experimental style. While in France, she was best known for her piano work. This piece catapulted her into the wider public consciousness for the first time. If you are interested in hearing this piece, there are endless renditions available today, with new musicians still enraptured by Louise's composition.

## *Louise's Musical Accolades*

Though Louise was largely overlooked in her time, she still gained some formal recognition for her talent. She was awarded the Prix Chartier by the Académie des Beaux Arts twice, first in 1861 and again in 1869 (Duchen, 2021). The Prix Chartier is a musical composition award that focuses on the talents of chamber musicians. Louise was the first-ever recipient of this award, alongside Charles Dancla. The award was given out every year until 1942. Louise was one of only three women ever to be awarded the prize. The next female recipient wouldn't come until 1890.

# Louise and Feminism

There is no doubt that Louise was more acclaimed than many of her male contemporaries who worked at the Paris Conservatoire. Her studies became compulsory for piano students, and she inspired young minds through her unconventional approach to music. She was a true visionary—and yet, she was still paid far less than the male professors. Louise was incensed by this. She fought and argued for her right to equal pay for 10 years. This uproar could have led to her being fired from the conservatory, although her talent was far too great for them to let her go. She leveraged all the power she had to continue her plight.

It wasn't until her piece "Nonet" gained popularity in the 1850s that she was finally granted equal pay. The men could no longer ignore her contribution to the school—and to the musical world as a whole. She was surrounded by men all the time. She was constantly being told that she wasn't equal—now she had found a way to make them recognize her true worth.

## Louise's Legacy

The truest testament to Louise's influence on music is that her pieces are still being performed today. She's been recognized by popular media, such as the BBC, as one of the greatest composers of all time. You might not have noticed it, have a look around—her recordings are everywhere. While her work was largely forgotten in the 20th century, it has seen a resurgence in popularity and recognition over the last two decades.

Louise is also recognized as one of the most renowned professors to ever teach at the Paris Conservatoire, having influenced a whole slew of female students to pursue their passion and find their own success. And let's not forget how completely unique her style was: She promoted creativity and experimentation when so many just wanted to achieve fame. She and her husband created a music publishing house and an anthology of music that has shaped the knowledge of many modern historians. Louise had a "never give up" attitude. Even though she didn't receive the recognition afforded to her male contemporaries like Beethoven or Chopin, that didn't dampen her spirit. She always knew that her talent would speak for itself. She also wasn't driven by a need to be popular. Music and teaching made her happy and fulfilled. She was content with her life. I look at this as a reminder that external recognition is not everything. To really be happy, we need to recognize our talents within ourselves.

Additionally, Louise was one of the first prominent voices to demand equal pay. She laid the foundation for many other women to ask for the same. She proved that talent is enough, regardless of gender. Without women like her, the suffragette movement might not have started so soon after her death. She used her platform to show beyond doubt that women had talents to match—and exceed—those of men. It took her a decade to achieve her own equality, once again proving that she was never going to back down because things weren't going her way. Her lesson is one of perseverance. If you really want something, you need to keep aiming for it again and again. Change doesn't happen quickly—and we as women need to use our enormous aptitude for resilience to keep questioning and challenging inequalities. No matter how male-dominated the world is, our talents and voices can rise above.

# 3

## DAME ETHEL SMYTH (1858-1944)

In the midst of the suffragette movement in the United Kingdom, one musical woman stood out as an icon. Dame Ethel Smyth is remembered not only for her contribution to orchestral works, chamber music, piano talents, and opera writing—she is also remembered for being a tireless contributor to the fight for equal rights. Ethel was an eccentric character and has even been referred to as a "wild child" (Buzacott, 2021). She surrounded herself with powerful women and was truly a force of nature. As you can imagine, she was often overshadowed by her male contemporaries, although that never discouraged her. The British royal family officially recognized her talents when she was awarded a damehood. In fact, Ethel was the first female composer to ever become a dame (Phinney, 2018).

Ethel was born smack-dab in the middle of a growing suffragette movement in England. It started in 1832, 26 years before she was born, and continued throughout her lifetime. In the 19th century, women of all ages were destined to serve the men in their lives through domestic duties. They wore the infamous crinoline, which is a huge bell-shaped skirt (Hughes, 2014). Historians note that this outfit was incredibly constrictive and made it impossible for women to perform tasks like sweeping stairs without falling over (Hughes, 2014). The men of the time held the notion that women were inferior, and the two genders lived in separate spheres from one another. Girls were usually married off in their early 20s to men who were at least five years their senior. They were expected to be chaste until marriage, and while they were expected to find a husband, it was deemed as improper for these women to actively seek a partner. Indeed, it was all up to the men to decide who they wanted them to marry. It is no wonder that women started to fight back. They wanted equal pay, the right to vote and to own property, and they wanted to have control over their own finances.

Ethel was a passionate believer that women were not inferior to men. She used her music to write a composition that was adopted as the anthem of the suffragettes. She aligned herself with the most influential women of the time and was an integral part of the fight.

One of the most interesting parts of Ethel's story is her personality. Not many women of her time are remembered for their tenacity, b Ethel is considered to be a vibrant example of how women have always been multifaceted—even if men tried to dull her down. Now, I know that this is something that still happens to women in the modern era. Oftentimes, we are expected to be meek or silent in order to fit in. One of the great joys of my life is simply watching females outshine males. Women are funny, exciting, and intelligent—we should never have to minimize our personalities to conform to what society expects from us.

Ethel continuously found ways to rail against the patriarchy. She used her talent as a musician to stand out, and her story absolutely deserves to be told. While her works were not accepted into the mainstream of the early 20th century, her legacy lives on today as one of the most important people to shape music. I find her tenacity inspirational, and I'm sure you will, too.

## A Brief History

Ethel Smyth was born on the 22nd of April, 1858, in Sidcup, England. Her father, Major-General John Hall Smyth, was a general in the Royal Artillery, and it is presumed that her mother, Emma Struth Smyth, was a homemaker. Ethel was the fourth of eight children in her family. She would write about her parents, reflecting on her father as a strict authoritarian who often beat his children for infractions and misbehaving (Simkin, 2014). She adored her mother, who was a kind and gentle spirit. It was her mother who introduced her to music. Ethel writes that Emma

Smyth "was in fact one of the most naturally musical people I have ever known" (Simkin, 2014).

When Ethel was around 10 years old, her father received a promotion, and the family moved into a large house in Frimley Green, where they were able to employ servants. Ethel would spend her early childhood riding through town on her bicycle, often with a cigarette in her mouth (Buzacott, 2021). As the family was now upper-class, her behavior was deemed completely improper. She also started talking about her dreams of becoming a composer—another thing that was deemed improper. Her father was outraged by his daughter's rebellious attitude and ambition and sent her to boarding school to straighten her out.

This did not dampen Ethel's spirit, however. Against the wishes of her father, she enrolled in the Leipzig Conservatory, where she started to study music at age 18. She was taught by famed composer Alexander Ewing, who introduced her to some of the most popular and renowned music of the time, including the works of Wagner. After a year at the conservatory, Ethel found that she wasn't getting enough attention from her tutors. They favored male students over her, and she was seldom allowed to perform or write her own compositions. She left the institution and began studying under the tutelage of Heinrich von Herzogenberg. Henrich was an Austrian composer and conductor who was very influential at the time. Interestingly, historians note that Ethel far outshone her teacher's success, as he is barely remembered for his work today.

While in Leipzig, Ethel encountered many other famous musicians, such as Russian composer Pyotr Ilyich Tchaikovsky who wrote some of the most popular theatrical pieces of music of the Romantic era. She also met Clara Schumann, who she considered as "one of the few women composers whom one can seriously consider to be achieving something valuable in the field of musical creation" (Wilcox-Lee, 2014).

Surrounded by so much great talent, Ethel was able to build on her own skills. She wrote one of her first works, "String Quartet no. 1," whilst in Leipzig. She then began to travel across Europe, learning about different styles of music. She met poets and musicians alike, and word of her talent began to spread. People were entranced with Ethel's ability to compose and perform. Nonetheless, she was still overlooked by many of her male contemporaries.

# Ethel and Music

Ethel returned to Frimley Green in 1885 at the age of 27. By this time, she was already recognized as an acclaimed composer across Europe. She had a collection of influential friends who supported her ventures, including the Empress of France, Eugenie de Montijo. Her connection to the Empress led to greater things. Eugenie invited Ethel to visit Balmoral, one of the residences of the British royal family. While visiting, Ethel performed her piece "Mass in D" in front of Queen Victoria. This led to the piece receiving financial backing and recognition, and in 1893, it was performed at the famous Royal Albert Hall and was widely published across the continent (Buzacott, 2021).

Despite her popularity, male composers sought to tear Ethel down. Her music was described as "energetic, loud, [and] forceful," and it was deemed as "unbecoming of a woman" (D'Silva, 2022). She had overwhelming support from music lovers, alas, her male contemporaries were still not fans. They began to call her a "lady composer" to take away from her credibility. They thought that her sound was too masculine and that she should write softer music that appealed more to women.

Ethel wasn't in the least bit deterred. In 1898, at age 40, she changed tact and started writing for the opera, which was incredibly popular in the late 19th century and early 20th century. Her first and second opera pieces, "Fantasio," and "Der Wild," were performed in Germany before making their way to the Royal Opera House of Covent Garden in the UK (Buzacott, 2021). Her music started to make its way out of Europe and received acclaim in North America as well.

### *The Wreckers*

Ethel Smyth's most famous piece of opera composition was "The Wreckers," written between 1902 and 1904 in conjunction with composer Henry Brewster. Tim Ashley, a classical and opera critic, writes:

Smyth presents us with an at times chilling portrait of a devout yet hypocritical Cornish community plundering ships lured onto nearby rocks, only to find its skewed values challenged when Thurza, the disaffected wife of the pastor Pasko, begins an affair with the fisherman Marc (2022).

"The Wreckers" has been described as a "feminist opera" by modern-day critics (D'Silva, 2022). They note that the central theme is about a woman trying to find her voice and overcome the stereotype that women need to be saved by men.

The three-part opera is described as stylistically inventive and a collection of a mix of influences of the time (Ashley, 2022). It is still performed to this day across the globe. Each new rendition of the performance breathes a fresh perspective into a piece that is over a century old. Ethel's name has not been forgotten due to the enduring nature of "The Wreckers." The fact that this opera still has relevance in today's musical landscape is astounding.

## ETHEL AND SEXUALITY

The concept of sexuality in relation to Ethel Smyth's life has been widely discussed by researchers and music fans alike. First, there is the fact that Ethel formed an intimate relationship with Henrich's wife, Lisl. There are some unfounded theories that the two women fell in love. This is not documented by any historians, although is rather a popular theory among fans of Ethel's work.

Additionally, it is said that Ethel and Henry became lovers during their time working together. Researchers at *Music by Women* theorize that "He was her only male partner; Smyth preferred the company of women throughout her life" (Music by Women, 2021). This, of course, adds a little fuel to the fire regarding her relationship with Lisl von Herzogenbergs.

Another writer notes that Ethel was a good friend and "possible lover" of some of the most famous women of the 20th century, including suffragette Emmeline Pankhurst and prolific writer Virginia Woolf (Broad,

2020). In fact, Ethel wrote about her relationship with Virginia Woolfe, saying, "I don't think I have ever cared for anyone more profoundly" (D'Silva, 2022).

Professor Sophie Fuller, a music lecturer at Trinity Laban Conservatoire of Music and Dance, is certain that Ethel was queer. She writes that Ethel was "as open as anyone of her generation could be about the intense, and sometimes sexual, relationships with women that drove so much of her often-turbulent life" (D'Silva, 2022).

With homosexuality being a taboo topic in the early 20th century, there is no way to know for certain if Ethel was, in fact, taking both male and female lovers throughout her life. The stories of many female lovers have been lost to history because they couldn't be formally documented at the time. I leave it up to you to decide what you think is the true story here.

## ETHEL AND THE SUFFRAGETTE MOVEMENT

Ethel Smyth's disillusionment with the concept of femininity started at an early age. She was a crass child who wanted to do as she pleased. Throughout her musical career, she dressed in a way similar to a man, donning tweed jackets and trousers. She wrote whatever kind of music she liked, never conforming to the idea that women could only write chamber music—though it must be said that her foray into chamber music was incredibly well regarded. She wrote in different styles and experimented in a way that no other woman of her era was doing. With her sexuality being ambiguous in nature, she paved the way for women to experiment with love in different ways. The fact that she never married provided evidence that women could survive without male companionship. All of this was a precursor to her participation in the suffragette movement.

In 1910, Ethel met Emmeline Pankhurst, and the two developed a strong relationship. Ethel wrote about Emmeline, saying this meeting was "the fiery inception of what was to become the deepest and closest of relationships" (D'Silva, 2022). She was inspired to join the feminist movement and even stopped writing operas to follow her passion for bringing equal rights to women. In 1911, at age 53, she wrote "The March of Women," which is now heralded as the anthem of the suffragette movement in England.

Ethel was a disruptor. She didn't do anything in half-measures. In 1912, she was one of more than 100 other women who were arrested for property damage to the Houses of Parliament during a protest. She was sent to Holloway Prison for two months, where she and Emmaline had adjoining cells. In the cells, the arrested women would sing "The March of Women" to pass the time. The conditions were horrible. The prison was damp, there were cockroaches filling the cells, and still, the women found power in Ethel's music. Ethel was released after three weeks, likely due to the connections she had made throughout her life to powerful men and women.

## ETHEL'S LEGACY

With her compositions still being performed today, it is safe to say that Ethel Smyth has not been forgotten by music lovers. Her works transcend time and place, and stagings of her opera are still popular into the 2020s. Her penchant for making friends and her unusual personality was remembered by all those who encountered her. She is regarded as a unique person who never conformed to societal pressure.

Late in her life, Ethel spent time reflecting on her legacy, and decided to capture this by writing memoirs. One passage could sum up her contribution to the world, it would probably be this:

I generally dress in tweeds, and sometimes, at winter afternoon concerts, have even conducted them; because I was a militant suffragette and seized a chance of beating time to 'The March of the Women" from the window of my cell in Holloway Prison with a tooth brush; because I have written books, spoken speeches, broadcast, and don't always make sure that my hat is on straight; for these and other equally pertinent reasons, in a certain sense I am well known (Buzacott, 2021).

We can all use Ethel's legacy as inspiration in our own lives. She fought for her rights, she didn't give up when men tried to tell her she wasn't talented, and she lived boldly and proudly as herself. She didn't dull her own light and never let anybody else do so either. Ethel's story got me thinking; Why should we ever be anybody other than our authentic selves? We are all fascinating women who bring intelligence, laughter, and fresh perspectives to the lives of others. Dame Ethel Smyth made dozens of friends on her travels, proving that if you just be yourself, people will gravitate toward you. There is no reason to give up or not stand up for what you believe in. If a woman in the early 20th century could do it, so can you.

# 4

## NELLIE MELBA (1861-1931)

Ethel Smyth isn't the only dame to make an extraordinary impact on music. Nellie Melba was a renowned Australian operatic soprano during the Victorian era. In her time, she was one of the most famous singers both in her home country and worldwide. Notably, she was the first Australian classical performer to achieve international success. There is an almost endless list of awards and accolades that Nellie achieved in her lifetime. Perhaps most impressive is the fact that her portrait is featured on the $100 note in Australia; on the other side of the bill is the First World War general Sir John Monash. She is the only female musician to be featured on this currency. I think that is proof enough that Nellie Melba was an incredibly influential figure and remains so to this day.

Australian women struggled in the 19th century. Similarly to the previous stories from France and England, women had very few legal rights. They were expected to marry—and once they had a husband, their rights were limited even further, as they were then transferred into the hands of their husbands, including all property and any wages they earned (National Museum of Australia, 2012). As mothers, these women didn't have any legal guardianship over their children, and a child could be removed from their care at any given time. Before 1870, women could also not file for divorce (National Museum of Australia, 2012). If they worked, they were paid two-thirds less than their male counterparts. Due to this inequity, there was a budding movement by women to make a change. In the year that Nellie was born, 1861, South Australia changed its laws to allow women who owned property to vote. Nellie's home state of Victoria didn't pass the same law until 1908 and was the last to do so in the country. There was a change in the tides— it was coming slowly.

Women were gaining more access to education, and 1903 marked the first instance of a woman running in the federal election.

Throughout her life, Nellie saw women rise up against the patriarchy. And she was determined to make a name for herself despite male musicians being much more popular (and much better paid). The names of many of those men have been forgotten, though the legacy left by Nellie is strong to this day.

Nellie was tenacious. She was rebellious from a young age and stood up for herself when needed. She also battled with feelings of being misunderstood and went through great bouts of depression and anxiety. I think this is something that we all experience; while it's common for women to push down their feelings and try to persevere through heartache, I think Nellie is an example of how we are allowed to feel our emotions and how we can still be successful even when we are struggling. Nellie was also plagued by a need to be accepted and praised—doesn't that sound familiar? I know it's uncouth to admit that we want people to see our talents and praise us for them, it's a basic human instinct! Nellie's story demonstrates to us that while the opinions of others don't define us, it's okay to want people to see us as talented, smart, or capable. Nellie also struggled with criticism. Don't we all! However, she used the feedback (even if it was wrong) to strive toward greater success. Negative opinions can indeed spur us on to be better. There is no greater feeling of satisfaction than proving people wrong.

Nellie's contribution to music is incredibly impressive. She shone brightly and is still considered to be one of Australia's greatest performers. She traveled the world and caught the eye of countless music lovers.


## A Brief History

Before Nellie changed her name, she was Helen Porter Mitchell. Born on the 19th of May, 1861, in Richmond, Victoria, she was the eldest of seven children. Prior to her birth, her father, David Mitchell, and mother, Isabella Ann Mitchell, unfortunately, lost two children who died in infancy. David Mitchell emigrated to Australia from Scotland in 1852 and made a name for himself as a builder. He was renowned in his own right, with one of his projects, the Royal Exhibition Building, becoming the first structure in Australian history to be named a UNESCO World Heritage site. David built the large family home where his children grew up, dubbing it "Doonside."

Nellie learned piano and started singing in public at just six years old. Immediately, her talent was recognized as otherworldly. She had a heavenly voice and strong piano skills. She would eventually go on to learn how to play the church organ as well.

Nellie described herself as being "an unusually naughty child: incorrigible, unreasonable and unmanageable, incapable of behaving even by accident" (Wainwright, 2021). This displeased her father greatly. He was a God-fearing man who greatly disapproved of his daughter's rebellious attitude. Meanwhile, her mother was a musical woman—she was Nellie's first teacher.

As she got older, she was sent to a strict boarding school which she loathed. Here, her parents hoped that she would become a more docile woman. In her teenage years, she began performing at amateur concerts and in church.

She then went on to study at the Presbyterian Ladies College, where she studied music. Her father encouraged her to take up musical ,studies although he didn't want her to be a performer. He believed performing would lead her to be promiscuous (Wainwright, 2021). While at college, Nellie was taught by renowned singer Manuel Garcia. When she finished school, she continued her lessons with Pietro Cecchi, who had studied at Rome's Academy of Music. She was surrounded by impressive men who had reached musical acclaim, and she wanted to be just like them.

When Nellie was 20, tragedy struck the Mitchell family. Her mother died from a battle with chronic hepatitis and liver failure. Prior to her death, she made her oldest child promise that she'd look after the baby of the family, four-year-old Vere. When Vere became sick from a chest infection, Nellie reportedly had a mystical experience. She saw her mother, dressed in the clothes she was buried in, sitting in the room. This led her to believe that something terrible was going to happen to her little sister. She told her father, who dismissed her concerns. He delayed having a doctor come to see Vere, and unfortunately, his youngest daughter choked to death overnight (Wainwright, 2021). In the span of three months, Nellie had lost two of her closest and most beloved family members. Nellie was wracked with guilt over both deaths, and her father noticed the emotional toll it was taking on her. He decided to get her out of Doonside, taking her on a business trip to the Queensland town of Mackay, some 1,200 miles from her home in 1881.

Nellie, now 21, found Mackay fascinating. It had a thriving culture and a love for music, and she soon became a staple singer and piano player in the town. She was also growing into a woman. One writer describes her as having the olive skin of her mother and that she was "handsome rather than pretty, with dark, almond-shaped eyes and a fine-lipped mouth that seemed lost between a long, distinctive nose and prominent oval chin" (Wainwright, 2021). She garnered the attention of many males in Mackay, although she was interested in one in particular—Charlie Armstrong.

### An Unfortunate Marriage

Charlie was the son of an Irish baron and politician who died when his son was five. Charlie spent the rest of his life working odd jobs and eventually settling on farm work. The pair were not suited on paper. Nellie was a city girl and a dreamer, and Charlie was completely disinterested in music and loved the countryside. Charlie also had a temper, which her father was worried about. Still, he gave his blessing, and in 1882, Nellie and Charlie married. Nellie quickly became disenfranchised with the notion of marriage. The pair lived in a tin-roofed house that echoed the sound of constant rain, which only made Nellie more frustrated (Davidson, 2006). She missed the city. To make matters worse, Charlie was also physically abusive, beating Nellie on more than one occasion.

The pair had a son together, George, in 1883, less than a year into their marriage. The child did little to quash the issues between the couple. Nellie still dreamed of a career as a singer and ultimately left her husband in 1884. She returned to Melbourne to pursue her passion.

## NELLIE AND MUSIC

Upon her return to Melbourne, Nellie resumed her performing with vigor. She was determined now to make a name for herself. Nellie made her debut at a Liedertafel concert at the Melbourne Town Hall in her first year back in the city (Davidson, 2006). Her talent was written about by Australian music critics who were incredibly impressed by her operatic singing. That night, she met John Lemmone, who ended up being a lifelong friend and collaborator (Davidson, 2006). She started to see some success in her home city and had bigger aspirations.

David Mitchell was also experiencing success. He was appointed as commissioner to the Indian and Colonial Exhibition, which took him to London in 1886. Nellie accompanied her father on the trip, hoping for international acclaim. Her English debut at the London Princes' Hall was not well received. This was a massive setback, particularly for a woman who struggled with criticism. Nellie had grown accustomed to being beloved by the public and critics alike. She kept trying, though. She got in touch with Sir Arthur Sullivan, begging for a part of his opera, although this time was not successful. Arthur told her that she needed to continue studying and that if she improved, he might offer her a small role (Davidson, 2006).

She took his advice and moved to Paris, where she started lessons with Mathilde Marchesi, A German mezzo-soprano. Mathilde was a prominent teacher on the scene, and her opinion mattered. She had an eye for spotting talent and saw great promise in Nellie. The two women worked well together, and at the end of 1886, Mathilde invited Nellie to perform the "Mad Scene" in Ambroise Thomas's rendition of *Hamlet* (Klein, 1931).

Her quick progression caught the eye of Maurice Strakosch, an impresario (which means someone who handles the finances for operas and plays). He signed her on a 10-year contract. This, however, was short-lived. Maurice died in 1887, leaving Nellie free to take on an even better offer from the Theatre de la Monnaie in Brussels.

In October of 1887, Nellie made her operatic debut at the theater as the character Gilda in *Rigoletto*. She went on to perform in several more operas, including the famous *La Traviata* and *Lucia di Lammermoor*.

Nellie's success in Brussels led her to gain more and more roles. She was still upset about her experience in England and had little interest in returning to the country. She bit the bullet, though, and returned in 1888, where she once again performed as Lucia in *Lucia di Lammermoor*. Once again, she was met with lackluster reviews. She returned to Brussels, and then went on to Paris, making her Parisian debut as Ophelia in *Hamlet* in 1889. Here, she was met with overwhelming support from the public and critics. Over the course of her performances, she caught the eye of Lady de Grey, an influential figure in the opera world. She had great sway over performances at Covent Garden and begged Nellie to play a role in *Romeo et Julliette*. Her third foray onto the British scene was far more successful, and her star status continued to rise.

Covent Garden was in its golden age when Nellie performed there. She caught the eye of another impresario, Sir Augustus Harris, who was arguably the most important person in opera at the time. He had connections all over Europe and was a regular in royal circles. Nellie found his status and closeness to the most influential people in the world exhilarating. She wanted to perform for them. She wanted to perform for everyone.

### *How She Became Nellie Melba*

Now, this is just a quick aside. There isn't much to the story of how Nellie changed her name or why she did it. Like many before (and after) her, she wanted to adopt a stage name. Nellie may have wanted to shed her past identity and any past criticism (particularly her failure in London). She changed her name under the advisement of Mathilde Marchesi, and in 1887 as she was debuting in Brussels, she became known as Nellie Melba.

The surname Melba was a nod to her home city of Melbourne.

## *Nellie and High Society*

Another quick aside that I have to mention is how prominent Nellie became in high society. This is in large part due to her friendship with Lady de Grey. Abandoning her childhood rebellion, Nellie acted as though she was born into royalty. She was reportedly on a first-name basis with all the most influential royals of the last 19th century.

High society was entranced with her talent. According to author Jim Davidson, Nellie "had sung in Stockholm before King Oscar II, in Vienna before Emperor Franz Joseph, and in Berlin before Kaiser Wilhelm II; she had also been commanded by Queen Victoria to Windsor" (Davidson, 2006). She was endlessly financed by prominent European characters and lived lavishly. She was so successful (and rich) that she employed French workers to remodel her house after Versailles (Davidson, 2006).

## *An Affair*

An anecdote that I simply cannot leave out of Nellie's story is her affair with Prince Philippe, Duke of Orleans. Nellie was still technically married to Charlie Armstrong, and he had come to visit his wife and son. To occupy himself, he joined the army there. Though, this was also short-lived. Before Nellie debuted in Brussels for the first time, the married couple had a massive fight. He didn't want his wife to perform, and she wasn't going to be stifled. After this, he left, and the two were plainly done with each other.

Fast-forward to 1890, when Prince Philippe enters the scene. He was a French royal who lived in London. The pair were spotted all across Europe together and weren't exactly discrete about their affair. When Nellie traveled to perform for Tsar Nicholas II in Saint Petersburg, Philippe accompanied her. The press picked up the story of their relationship, which led, of course, to Charlie finding out. He filed for divorce immediately on the grounds of adultery, naming Philippe as a co-respondent (Davidson, 2006). The divorce was not granted, most likely due to diplomatic pressure from Philippe's people.

Regardless, it was undeniably a scandal. A royal and a performer—how wild! It drew so much attention that Philippe went on a two-year safari in Africa without Nellie to subdue the press.

Nellie and Charlie finally divorced in 1900 when he and their son, George, were living in Texas.

## *Nellie—The Star of the 1900s*

While her affair was happening, Nellie certainly didn't allow love to slow her down. As I mentioned, she went on to perform for the Russian Royal Family and continued to travel. Her 1893 performance as Nedda in *Pagliacci* at Covent Garden was a hit. An archived newspaper piece notes that the composer of *Pagliacci* was present at this performance and that he said he had never seen the role played so well (The New York Times, 1893).

In the same year, Nellie traveled to New York to make her American debut. She performed at the Metropolitan Opera House, a world-renowned venue. Through the rest of the 1890s, Nellie continued to perform at Covent Garden. I can't even list all her roles. Some notable ones include Aida in *Aida*, Violette in *La Traviata*, the titular role of *Helene*, and Desdemona in *Othello*.

By the 20th century, Nellie was an international star. And she was making good money. Thanks to the suffragette movements across the globe, she was able to keep her money and support herself as an independent woman. In the wake of her divorce with her former husband and son now living in Texas, she decided it was time to return home for a concert tour in 1902. This was a huge earning opportunity, with the profits described as unprecedented (Shawe-Taylor, 2001). One report claims that she made £21,000 during the tour (Davidson, 2006). She toured Australia and New Zealand between 1902 and 1903. Her local audience greeted her with overwhelming support. She was everything people wanted to be—glamorous, successful, and a star.

She wasn't home for good. In 1904, Nellie's presence was commanded by the French president, and she performed for him at Buckingham Palace. She went on to Monte Carlo to perform in *Helene* between 1906 and 1907. Nellie was in her 40s at this stage, and she was still going strong.

She went back to New York, then back to Australia in 1909 for another tour.

She continued to perform at Covent Garden frequently. In 1914, she celebrated her 25th anniversary at the venue. Nellie commemorated this achievement with a gala performance. It's said that there were at least seven kings and queens in attendance (Davidson, 2006).

With World War I starting in 1914, it became difficult for Nellie to continue performing. After the war, she returned to Covent Garden, and things were different now. The people of England—and all over—were despondent after the massive loss of life.

She returned to Australia in 1922 and held two massive concerts in Melbourne and Sydney. Approximately 70,000 people came to see her perform (Davidson, 2006). She ensured that the price of the tickets was cheap enough so that all types of people could attend.

### *The Farewell*

In 1926, at age 65, Nellie performed a farewell concert at Covent Garden. She returned to Australia to do another farewell concert. Then, she kept doing farewell concerts. People theorize that the massive number of attendees who came to her farewells bolstered her self-esteem, and she just couldn't stop (Davidson, 2006). In Australia, this is called "doing a Melba" (Davidson, 2006).

Her actual final Australian performance came in 1928 at the age of 67 in Melbourne. She continued to travel, and this included an ill-fated trip to Egypt. She developed a fever that she was never able to recover from. She went to Sydney for medical care and died in 1931 of septicemia. The entire globe mourned her death, and her funeral was a national event in Australia.

## NELLIE'S LEGACY

While Nellie was a prolific performer, she was also a philanthropist—for which she is also remembered. During World War I, Nellie raised

£100,000 for the Belgian war effort and for charities in Australia. Nellie lost five family members during the war.

In 1918, she was made a dame—not for her music, although for her charity work.

Nellie is remembered by musicians for her almost perfect vocal cords. She sang in three octaves. There is a marble bust of Nellie at Covent Garden, and she was inducted into the Victorian Honour Roll of Women in 2001 (Her Place Museum, 2010).

Anecdotally, Nellie has four types of food named after her, most famously Peach Melba—a dessert that's popular across the world. Google has celebrated her birthday via Google Doodles, and the University of Melbourne's musical hall is referred to as "Melba Hall."

In her lifetime, Nellie continuously confronted criticism and fought to prove her worth. She didn't back down in the face of critics and the public, and she went on to be one of the most famous opera singers of all time. She's proof that if you believe in yourself, you will be successful. She didn't allow overwhelming grief or an abusive marriage to dampen her dreams, and she proved that you can overcome anything if you are dedicated enough. Who would have thought that a girl from Melbourne could become one of the biggest names around the world? Nellie's perseverance and strength are something I find so inspiring.

# 5

## Bessie Smith (1894-1937)

### Empress of the Blues

Known as the "Empress of the Blues," Bessie Smith was a force to be reckoned with. In fact, Bessie is *still* a force to be reckoned with. Though gone, her impact on music has lived on, having a long-lasting effect on singers for generations, and her style will never be forgotten. Bessie's life was not an easy one— her spirit and determination never wavered. She put all her frustrations with the world into her music. Scholars now consider her songs as some of the earliest examples of African-American protest music (Rabaka, 2012). She expressed the plight and struggles of an entire generation of people who were experiencing oppression and mistreatment, and to this day, her themes and lyrics are extremely relevant. Her life came to a startling short end before she could continue making changes in the world, and her legacy unquestionably lives on.

African-American women are often overlooked by history when examining the suffragette movement—although this is not because they weren't fighting for their rights. In fact, African-American women were some of the loudest and most tenacious protestors and activists in the United States. Not only were these women facing widespread inequality based on their gender, they were also experiencing rampant racism. African-American women were perhaps the most oppressed (and, unfortunately, this is still true in today's day and age). Prior to Bessie's birth, there was a growing movement across the country where African-American women were starting to rally against societal expectations of them. They wanted to align themselves with the white suffragettes. Perhaps the most famous example of this is an 1851 speech by former slave Sojourner Truth, entitled "Ain't I a Woman." Sojourner delivered her historical speech at a national women's rights convention in Ohio, and her example was followed by many other women across the country. Fast-forward a few decades to when Bessie was growing up in the early 1900s, the movement was still in its infancy, despite all the speeches and protests. In 1913, the first African-American women's suffrage club was formed in Chicago. African-American women became prominent figures in the fight for women's rights to vote—though in 1920, when the 19th Amendment was passed, the right to vote was not extended to any women of color. It wasn't until 1965 that African-American women were given the same rights. Keep in mind that segregation in the United States didn't end until 1964, almost 30 years after Bessie passed away.

All this is to say that Bessie's entire life was an uphill battle against sexism and racism. Bessie had few contemporaries with who she could see herself. Therefore, she took inspiration from the women who had come before her and started paving her own way, looking to inspire millions after her. She used her voice to speak about social issues like poverty and inequality. Many white people saw her music as crude or distasteful, it was the African-American community who found solace in her songs, seeing their own plights finally getting explored in popular music.

There is so much to say about Bessie Smith. She was confident and bold. She didn't worry about what people thought of her and her music. She toyed with the notion of sexuality and sexual freedom, and is remembered for being fearless in the face of all those who opposed her. In a time when people were trying to silence African-American women, Bessie's voice cut through as a beacon of hope and promise that change was on its way. She reminds me of so many powerful women that I see in the world today. So often, we are told that we need to be more gentle and less angry, even if we are speaking up against injustice. There is a particular stigma for African-American women, who are pigeonholed into the stereotype of an "angry black woman." This ridiculous stigmatization removes the validity of women's voices and our right to be angry. Women like Bessie came before us to show that speaking out is okay. There will always be critics there will also always be supporters and devotees.

# A Brief History

Bessie Smith was born on the 15th of April, 1894, in Chattanooga, Tennessee. Her father, William Smith, was a baptist preacher and laborer, and her mother, Laura, was a homemaker. She was one of five siblings, though census data from the late 1890s isn't always accurate, particularly when documenting the lives of African-American families. Bessie's father died before she was old enough to remember him. When she was nine, her mother and one of her brothers also passed away. This left her oldest sister, Viola, to care for the children (Albertson, 2003). The family didn't have enough money to send the kids to school, so Bessie never received an education. Instead, she helped her sister run the house.

The Smiths lived in poverty. Viola was constantly under stress, trying to figure out how to feed the family. By the age of nine, Bessie knew that she needed to start helping out. She and her brother Andrew took to the streets of Chattanooga and started busking to earn some money. Bessie would sing and dance while Andrew would play guitar. They lived in the heart of the African-American community and took every penny they earned back to their home to help out the family. Some reports state that Bessie also performed at the Ivory Theater around this time, marking this her earliest debut.

When Bessie was 10, her oldest brother Clarence joined a traveling troupe owned by Moses Stokes. One might say performance was in the blood of all the Smith children. Clarence was able to send home some money, and Bessie was able to receive some schooling as a result. When her brother and the troupe returned to Chattanooga in 1912, he organized an audition for his little sister. While Bessie was already considered a very talented singer, she was hired as a dancer for the troupe. The reason was that the troupe already had a singer—this singer was Ma Rainey. If that name sounds familiar to you, it's because Ma Rainey herself is one of the biggest stars of blues music. She is perhaps the only person that Bessie could look up to.

While Ma didn't teach Bessie how to sing, she did show her how to be a performer. She had an incredible stage presence that Bessie admired and emulated in her own career. Bessie traveled with the troupe as part of the chorus line before she began performing her own act in 1913. This was when she truly started establishing herself as a singer. The troupe toured through the Southern states and along the East Coast, with Bessie gaining a reputation as a singer who must be seen—though, of course, her mentor Ma was the star. Bessie traveled with the troupe until 1915. In 1918, at age 24, Bessie started a duo with fellow singer Hazel Green, all the while still working on her solo act of blues and comedy (Gaston, 2017).

By the 1920s, Bessie Smith was a name on the tongues of blues lovers across the Southern United States.

## BESSIE AND MUSIC

As the world entered a new era, the music scene started to change. Singer Mamie Smith (no relation to Bessie) sold 100,000 copies of her blues record. The record industry recognized that there was a previously untapped market they hadn't catered to. As such, they started to make a push toward targeting music for the African-American community. This was perfect timing for Bessie Smith.

In 1923, Bessie signed a record deal in New York with the famed Columbia Records (Gaston, 2017). Frank Walker, the talent agent who signed her, thought that she was one of the best performers he had seen in years. She recorded her record, including songs "Downhearted Blues" and "Gulf Coast Blues" in the same year. "Downhearted Blues" sold between 780,000–800,000 copies in the first six months (Gaston, 2017), outselling Mamie by hundreds of thousands of records. This led to Bessie performing sold-out shows in the Midwest, North, and South of the US.

By 1924, Bessie was the highest-paid Black entertainer, earning $2,000 a week (Gaston, 2017). She had cemented herself as a star. She toured the country in her own railroad car, and her record label nicknamed her the

"Queen of the Blues." The press ran with this and changed her moniker to "Empress of the Blues," which stuck around.

Bessie began collaborating with other big names in the industry, the most famous being Louis Armstrong. By the time the pair met in 1925, Bessie had already recorded 50 songs. That year, they recorded "Saint Louis Blues" with Bessie singing and Louis on the cornet. This song was inducted into the Grammy Hall of Fame in 1993 (Rascón, 2022). Another popular song they collaborated on was "Reckless Blues" in the same year.

Bessie was a star on stage. She commanded a presence like no other. Maureen Mahon of NPR describes her by saying, "Her onstage costumes of gowns, wigs, plumes and elaborate headdresses communicated glamour and wealth, and she carried herself with a regal bearing that fit her nickname" (Mahon, 2019). Indeed, Bessie became a style icon of the 1920s. In contrast to the wealth and glamor she was portraying, her music spoke to the core of African-American issues. She sang about sexism, racism, and poverty. This connected her with working-class audiences, who saw their lives represented in her music.

One of her most poignant songs was recorded in 1927 in the wake of the Great Mississippi Flood. The flood affected the African-American community greatly, with over 200,000 people displaced from their homes with nowhere to go. Bessie poignantly finished her song "Back-Water Blues" with the line "Mmm, I can't move no more/There ain't no place for a poor old girl to go" (Smith, 1927). She had traveled through the state and seen its effects on the people. She spoke about the experience like no other musician had done.

Unsurprisingly, Bessie had critics. When she auditioned for Black Swan Records, she was told that she needed to stop singing out of spite and that she was too rough for a woman (George et al., 2013). They wanted someone with more gentle styling, who was less abrasive and less of a diva. Despite all the acclaim and money she had earned, the white public (and even some of her fans) still saw her as lower-class. Instead of altering herself to fit in with what they wanted, Bessie just got more brash and outspoken. She wasn't going to be silenced by anybody.

At the end of the day, Bessie was still respected. She was a top earner, a sought-after performer, and someone who didn't need to minimize herself to achieve success. She recorded 160 albums for Columbia and sold-out shows across the country.

## The Great Depression and Beyond

When the Great Depression hit the United States, Bessie's career came to a halt. Columbia could no longer afford to produce any new records. People didn't have the means to attend her shows. Additionally, sound in film had gained popularity in the mid-1920s, which impacted the music industry greatly. People were less likely to see performers and more likely to watch a film. It very nearly killed the music industry altogether. There was nothing for singers and performers to do during this dark time.

Bessie wasn't going to allow her talents to go to waste. Even if she couldn't sell out massive theaters anymore, she would still keep sharing her gift. She began to sing in small clubs across the country. She even made her way onto Broadway in 1929, where she was part of a short-lived musical, *Pansy*. The musical was not well received—although critics did note that Bessie's performance was outstanding. In that same year, she made her debut in the short film *St. Louis Blues* where she sang the title track and played herself. Unfortunately, this film was lost, with the only copy ever found destroyed by a white liberal group in 1950.

By the 1930s, radio exposure greatly determined the success of a musical artist. Unfortunately, many of Bessie's lyrics were censored, or she wasn't played at all due to her controversial topics. Additionally, blues music wasn't as popular—the Swing Era was coming into full effect. She revised some of her old music in an attempt to update it to the new style. In 1933, she recorded her last songs, including "Take Me for a Buggy Ride" and "Do Your Duty." Her swing-style songs were also a huge hit. Even though she was keeping up with the times, she was still seen as a blues artist, and Columbia dropped her from their roster. Nonetheless, Bessie continued to tour and draw big crowds everywhere she went.

## BESSIE AND SEXUALITY

In the US in the 1920s, a same-sex relationship was a criminal offense. This wasn't going to stop female blues singers from exploring the notion of sexuality. Researchers and writers alike have spent the last few decades dissecting the lyrics of Bessie Smith and Ma Rainey, outlining that many of their lyrics alluded to same-sex relationships and experimentation. Some of it wasn't so covert.

Bessie was married to a man in 1923 by the name of Jack Gee just as her star was rising. Reportedly, the marriage was marred by affairs, including a number of female partners for Bessie. However, the couple didn't divorce until 1929, when Bessie found out about Jack's affair with singer Gertrude Saunders. He had reportedly cared less about Bessie's affairs because of how much money and fame she had. She wasn't as forgiving.

Writers now say that Bessie was pretty openly bisexual and was a little promiscuous while on the road. She once got into a fight with her lover Lillian Simpson, reportedly yelling, "I got twelve women on this show, and I can have one every night if I want it" (Hix, 2013).

She also explored her sexuality through her music, perhaps most famously in her 1930 song "The Boy in the Boat," where she sang, "when you see two women walking hand in hand, just look 'em over and trying and understand: They'll go to those parties—have the lights down low—only those parties where women can go" (Hix, 2013). Notably, this song wasn't recorded; only performed for audiences. Now, sexuality experts look at the piece of music as an integral part of homosexual history. Bessie additionally had a song called "Empty Bed Blues" where she explored the relationship between a man and a woman, and in at least one performance, changed the lyrics to a relationship about two women (Day, 2017). Even by today's standards, that's pretty raunchy!

A guitarist who played for Ma Rainey believed that Ma and Bessie were actually involved for a period of time while they toured together. He recalled that neither woman was interested when a man would be talking to them and that they'd always be looking for each other (Day, 2017).

Bessie Smith is now considered a bisexual icon.

## Bessie's Legacy

Bessie Smith's life was tragically cut short in 1937 after she was involved in a car crash on the road between Tennessee and Mississippi. She was rushed to the hospital and passed away before she could regain consciousness. She was 42.

Despite the grandeur of her life, Bessie's grave was unmarked for decades. In 1970, world-famous singer and icon Janis Joplin, alongside Juanita Green (who had worked for Bessie as a child), paid for a tombstone to be erected with the inscription "the greatest blues singer in the world will never stop singing" (Sexton, 2022). Janis saw Bessie as an inspiration and credited Bessie for her own success.

Bessie Smith is remembered for her musical talent. Three of her songs have been inducted into the Grammy Hall of Fame in the years since her death. In 1980, she was inducted into the Blues Hall of Fame. In 1989, she was posthumously awarded the Grammy Lifetime Achievement Award. In that same year, she was inducted into the Rock and Roll Hall of Fame. In 1994, a postage stamp was circulated in commemoration of Bessie. Even today, artists are still rerecording her music, and her songs are still played on blues stations across the world. No matter how much time passes, her talent proves to be enduring.

Numerous books and movies have been written about Bessie's life. In 2015, Queen Latifah took on the titular role in the HBO film *Bessie*. The film was a success, earning four Primetime Emmy Awards and winning "Outstanding Television Movie." The film focuses on the minutiae of Bessie's life, including her sexuality. If you have some time, I'd suggest watching it!

Bessie's contribution to African-American culture, as well as the LGBTQI+ community, is enormous in nature. She provided people who were cast aside solace in her songs, and her brazen attitude and willingness to explore taboo topics paved the way for people to stand up for themselves and embrace who they are.

She reminds us that we do not have to be a product of our time. No matter what the norm is, we still have the power to be ourselves—even if people don't accept that. She was a loud and proud woman who did things on her own terms and kept pushing. Bessie started life as an orphan girl who came out of obscurity and achieved success. She leveraged her talent to support her family and, in turn, found success beyond her wildest dreams. Bessie shows us that no matter where you come from or what your early childhood is like, you have the strength to seize opportunities as they come and make something of yourself. So much of popular music and societal change is indebted to Bessie Smith. She is a true inspiration.

# 6

## BILLIE HOLIDAY (1915-1959)

### LADY DAY

One of the artists that Bessie Smith greatly influenced was the acclaimed Billie Holiday. Billie's name is synonymous with jazz music, and without her, the genre simply wouldn't be the same. Her career is marked by her unique vocal delivery and ability to improvise through music. She had numerous sell-out shows at the most famous music venues in the United States, recording some of the most influential songs of the past century. She was a complicated person, landing herself in legal trouble and even prison, and this just adds to the flair of who she was. She wasn't the perfect picture of a successful woman who did all the right things, nor did she need to be—she was multifaceted and eccentric. Billie is another example of an African-American woman who didn't allow racial discrimination to dampen her success. She proved that you can be talented and iconic no matter where you come from or what you look like.

When Billie was experiencing the peak of her career, segregation was rampant throughout the United States. When she was just a little girl, the Great Depression was sweeping the country and indiscriminately affecting the lives of all Americans. However, no group of people were hit harder by the economic collapse than African-Americans. Almost half of the African-American community was out of work during the 1920s, and typically, they were the first to be fired from jobs, no matter their experience or talent. In the following decade, racial violence began to rise. In 1933, there were 28 lynchings of African-American people, mostly in the Southern states (Library of Congress, 2021). The National Association for the Advancement of Colored People (NAACP) continued its plight to push for a federal anti-lynching law throughout the decade; however, the first year on record without an occurrence of lynching wasn't until 1952 (NAACP, 2021). Post World War II, the civil rights movement gained momentum. Famous activist Rosa Parks is credited with the beginning of the movement when she refused to move to the back of a bus in 1955 in Alabama, more on Rosa in an up coming book. This led to Martin Luther King, Jr. organized a bus boycott and eventually to the first desegregated bus line in the South. Still, countrywide segregation would not come to an end for another nine years. Once more, it's important to remember that African-American women were the last to receive voting rights in the United States. They remained the most ostracized community for decades after white women's suffrage laws were passed, and this is an enduring issue to this day.

Billie saw a great many world-altering events in her lifetime. From the Great Depression to another World War, she lived through some of the most defining moments in history. And she became a defining figure herself. Due to segregation, Billie would sometimes perform at clubs and then be refused service afterward because she wasn't white. She wrote protest songs and sang about the plight for equality. Her music spoke directly to the thousands of people across the country experiencing discrimination. Billie didn't shy away from topics that made people uncomfortable. She was always going to use her platform for a good cause.

Many of those who encountered Billie remember her fun and zesty personality. She was full of contradictions. She was sensitive and warm—she was also full of pride and confidence. She was a lover and a heartbreaker. She was both introverted and extroverted. Billie showed that a woman didn't need to be one way or another. She proved that women can be anything they want and that they don't have to make sense. In my own life, I've seen people be confused by my changing demeanor or attitude. I often feel as though women are expected to be consistent and not have a variety of different reactions to circumstances. Society wants to be able to predict how we'll feel about something—and how unfair is that? We are all allowed to express ourselves, regardless of how we feel and no matter how people think we should behave. Shy women are also allowed to be confident. Outspoken women are also allowed to want solitude. Billie Holiday has left us with a solid example of how we can behave and emote in whatever way we see fit. Who we are isn't predetermined by what other people think we should be like.

*Note: This story contains a brief mention of sexual abuse. Reader discretion is advised.*

## A Brief History

Billie Holiday was born Eleanora Fagan on the 7th of April, 1915, in Philadelphia. Her parents, Sadie Fagan and Clarence Holiday were unwed teenagers at the time of her birth. This was frowned upon at the time, and the pair received no financial support from either of their families to assist with the birth of their child. Clarence Holiday was also a musician, and when Billie was still a baby, he abandoned his family to pursue a career playing the banjo. Sadie went on to marry another man, although this only lasted two years.

Sadie made arrangements for Billie to live with her half-sister Eva in Baltimore and joined them there after some time. Her mother was largely absent during her childhood, and Eva and her mother-in-law Martha mostly raised her on their own. The lack of stability in her early years meant that her life was very difficult. She started to rebel as a result. At nine years old, Billie faced juvenile court for her consistent truancy. As a result, she was sent to a reform school and baptized to rid her of her sins. She spent almost a year there before returning to her mother's care. While Billie was away, Sadie had opened a restaurant in Baltimore, and the two of them worked long hours to keep the place running. Billie dropped out of school at 11 to help out (Nicholson, 1995).

On Christmas Eve in 1926, when Billie was just 11, her mother came home to find a neighbor, Wilbert Rich, attempting to rape her daughter. They were able to fight off the attacker and called the police to have him arrested. It turns out that Wilbert Rich was a serial rapist in the area, and he was charged on six counts. This would have been an incredibly harrowing experience for young Billie, and to make matters worse, the court began to question Sadie's ability to care for her child. Billie was returned to the care of the reform school during the trial and was once again baptized (Nicholson, 1995). Her second stint at the reform school was horrendous. She recalls in her autobiography that she wasn't permitted to sleep in the same dormitory as the other students, and at one point, she was locked into a room with a girl who had died (Wells, 2020a). To pass the time, Billie started singing to herself and the other girls.

In 1927, she returned back to her mother and continued working in the restaurant. She met some interesting characters at the restaurant, including the madame of a brothel, who employed Billie to help out with errands. She would wash basins and change towels, making some extra money to support her little family.

While this is an entirely horrible job for a child to have, it was a lightbulb moment for Billie. It was at the brothel that she first heard the music of Bessie Smith and Louis Armstrong and caught what she would later refer to as the "jazz bug" (Nicholson, 1995). She credits hearing Louis' song "West End Blues" as the moment she realized she loved music (Nicholson, 1995). She was also struck by Bessie Smith's emotional intensity and melodic style, which helped form her own style years down the track.

In 1928, Sadie was sick of Baltimore and moved to Harlem in New York City, leaving her daughter behind with Eva and Martha once more. Martha reportedly found it difficult to control young Billie, and the girl came and went as she pleased. She was working more and more at the brothel, meeting the clientele who endlessly fascinated her. Mondays were slow nights at the brothel, so to attract people into the venue, Billie started to perform. She listened to records by Bessie and Louis and developed a repertoire of songs to sing, learning the lyrics quickly and mastering their vocals with ease. She expanded her performances to other venues nearby.

The following year, Sadie sent for her daughter, and Billie moved to Harlem to join her mother. Sadie had begun sex work. At age 14, Billie, too, became a sex worker. In the same year, both mother and daughter were arrested for prostitution. Billie was sentenced to work at a hospital and workhouse for 100 days. During this time, Billie made up her mind. She said that she would "never scrub floors or keep house for white folks" ever again (Nicholson, 1995).

She was going to be a singer.

## BILLIE AND MUSIC

Billie, now a young teenager, set her sights on performance. However, before she got started, she wanted to rebrand herself (recall that, until now, she went by her birth name, Eleanora). She took the first name of Billie Dove, an actress she loved, and kept the surname of the father who had deserted her as a child. Thus, Billie Holiday was born. She first started performing with her neighbor Kenneth Hollan, who was a saxophone player. He had connections to clubs throughout Brooklyn, and the pair eventually found a regular spot at the Elk Club on Saturday nights. Simultaneously, Billie was also working with her mother in the kitchen of a restaurant called "Mexico," where she would assist with cooking and waiting tables. This is where Billie developed her skill of improvisation. She started to sing for tips from table to table, always changing the lyrics to her songs in order to provide a fresh experience for customers (Nicholson, 1995). She was coming up with new material on the spot and learning how to think quickly on her feet.

It was at this restaurant that Billie met Marge Johnson, who was headlining an act in a club on 7th Street. She secured Billie an audition. It was a daunting experience—Billie had never played at a club this large before. It hosted dancers and orchestras and was the hub of cultural activity. Billie was ultimately deemed too amateur, but she kept her head up. She took this as a lesson rather than a failure.

She continued performing with Kenneth Hollan at various clubs throughout Harlem and Brooklyn. Her reputation as a singer was growing. She spent all her time with other musicians, and would smoke marijuana and drink with them into the early hours of the morning. Billie was reportedly shy and quiet, although she was also entirely comfortable with inserting herself into the scene. She used this connection to learn about music. With the musicians, she would improvise her singing and focus on how to change her style depending on what they were playing.

Billie also bumped into her estranged father at this time. Clarence Holiday was playing in the Fletcher Band, and the father and daughter found themselves running in the same circles. However, they never got close. Too much had happened between them.

By age 17, Billie was able to secure herself a regular spot at Covan's, a popular New York club. She replaced singer Monette Moore, who had performed at the club for years and was an institution. It was a big role to fill. People were shocked to see a young Billie on stage instead of the regular performer. She was unique, and her ability to harmonize was well beyond her years. Monette Moore's reputation helped Billie greatly. In 1933, producer John Hammond came to see Monette and instead heard Billie sing for the first time. He was amazed and signed her to record two songs. At 18, Billie made her recording debut with "Your Mother's Son-in-Law" and "Riffin' the Scotch." In total, she sold just under 6,000 records.

Billie caught the eye of legendary jazz composer Duke Ellington, whom she collaborated with in 1934. Duke was creating a film short called *Sympathy in Black* and featured her on the song "Saddest Tale." He was amazed by her ability to convey emotion through three notes, creating a link between herself and the audience, even if the audience wasn't present. She seemed to have the ability to connect with the lyrics on a personal level and take on the character of the song (Nicholson, 1995). Her role in this marked her debut performance at the Apollo Theater and was just another step in the right direction for Billie's career.

While she was gaining acclaim, the world was still not gentle on Billie. She continued to experiment with drugs and alcohol. She was also still subject to the discriminatory laws of segregation. She would headline a performance at a club, she'd be the belle of the ball, and then she'd have to use the service elevators so that no white patrons would be upset (Wells, 2020a). She was often forced to eat alone in a dark room so that nobody would see her off-stage or mixing with any of the white band members (Wells, 2020a).

## Billie and the Bands

Billie didn't record another song in 1934, instead spending the year performing throughout the New York club scene. After her appearance at the Apollo, she caught the eye of Ralph Cooper, who was the master of ceremonies at the famed venue. He took a liking to Billie and wanted her to be part of his newly formed band. She would be a featured vocalist, and they performed across Harlem together.

As this was happening, another young woman was coming up on the scene. Her name was Ella Fitzgerald. Billie was immediately envious of the girl, who had gained a role as a vocalist for the Chick Webb Orchestra, a highly sought-after spot. Billie was reportedly very bitter and called Ella, a name I won't repeat, but it rhymes with "witch" (Davidson, 2006).

Two years after her first recording with John Hammond, Billie was signed to Brunswick to record with pianist Teddy Wilson in order to create swing-style music. The duo relied heavily on improvisation to create music and together made "What a Little Moonlight Can Do," "Twenty-Four Hours a Day," and "If You Were Mine" (Bogdanov et al., 2003). "What a Little Moonlight Can Do" was a huge success, and the record label saw that Billie had the ability to stand on her own two feet as an artist.

After this, Billie started recording as a solo artist, experimenting with jazz and swing. While the record label had given her the ability to make money from music, they weren't exactly doing her any favors. She recorded without contracts and was paid a flat fee, excluding royalties. When her songs would sell in the thousands, she wouldn't see any of that profit.

Before she was even in her 20s, Billie's stardom was skyrocketing. She started touring with the Count Basie Orchestra in 1937. During this tour, she developed her persona. She was going to be a woman unlucky in love. Some of her most famous songs from this era include "I Can't Get Started" and "I Must Have That Man." While recordings of Billie and the Count Basie Orchestra exist, she was not allowed to record with them in the same room.

While in the orchestra, Billie was once again confronted with Ella Fitzgerald and her growing fame. Their two bands were in direct competition with each other, creating similar music for the same audience. While Billie wasn't originally a fan of Ella, the two did become friends (Gourse, 1997). Nobody understood what they were going through in this crazy world other than each other.

There are a couple of different stories that explain the reason why Billie stopped performing with Count Basie and his band. Some say that the band found her to be temperamental. Others say that she left because she wasn't being paid an adequate wage and that they weren't letting her explore her style. No matter what the truth is (and both could be true), she moved on to other things. She was hired by bandleader Artie Shaw to perform alongside him. This made her the first African-American woman to work with a white band (Billie Holiday, 2019), leading to a rise in vitriol toward Billie. When the band toured the South, Billie would be heckled by the audience, who would scream slurs at her as she performed.

In 1938, at age 23, Billie and Artie Shaw were broadcast on the most powerful New York radio station, WABC, which served to increase their exposure in a newfound way. While they were seeing great success together, Billie was struggling immensely with the racial divide. She wasn't allowed to eat with the band or use the same elevators as them. Audiences complained about seeing her milling about after the performance in the "whites only" clubs. She was forced to enter and leave via the kitchen so that she remained unseen by anybody until she was on stage. She left the band after just one year with them. The only record they created together was "Any Old Time."

After her stint with the two bands, Billie became known all over the country for her talent. Her 1938 song "I'm Gonna Lock My Heart" was the sixth most-played song in September of that year, and it peaked at number two on the charts that year (Nicholson, 1995).

### Strange Fruit

Billie Holiday's popularity reached its highest point in 1939 when she independently recorded her song "Strange Fruit." She was recording for Columbia Records at the time, and they refused to publish the songs themselves. Billie performed the song for Commodore label heads and moved them to tears with how brilliant it was. Columbia agreed to give her a single session release so that she could make this record.

"Strange Fruit" is so important and so poignant because it explores the lynching of African-Americans during that time. It was written originally by Lewis Allen before it made its way to Billie. In 1939, it was considered to be a graphic and brutal portrayal of the violence, and it made Billie a part of race relations tensions in a way that she had never experienced before.

Though the civil rights movement wouldn't gain its full momentum for several more years, this song is considered to be the precursor for what was to come. Billie was now a name known by people in the government, who weren't happy with her creating protest music. This would lead her to bigger issues, there's more on that later.

## *Lady Day*

The 1940s saw Billie Holiday gain commercial success. In 1941, she recorded one of her most popular songs, "God Bless the Child," with Arthur Herzog. In her autobiography, Billie says that the inspiration for the song came after she had an argument with her mother about money. Billie had been supporting Sadie financially, and when Billie found that she needed some of the money back from her mother, Sadie refused. Billie reportedly yelled, "God bless the child that's got his own," and that's how the song was born (Holiday & Dufty, 2011). This song is now part of the Grammy Hall of Fame.

Billie was still under a contract with Columbia at this time and wanted to experiment elsewhere, so she donned the name "Lady Day" to record "Trav'lin Light" with Capitol Records in 1942. This song performed well commercially, peaking at number five on the charts.

At 29, Billie signed with Decca Records and recorded "Lover Man," another one of her smash hits. This is where she became a real pop star, if one would apply that term. She was creating commercially successful tracks that the whole country was singing along to.

It was around this time (or perhaps even in the late 1930s; the timeline isn't 100% accurate) that Billie met Frank Sinatra. He was entranced with her performances and singing and would later say, "It is Billie Holiday... who was, and still remains, the greatest single musical influence on me" (Copeland, 2021).

Billie had married trombonist Jimmy Monroe in 1941, though it was not a happy marriage. By 1946, she released the song "Don't Explain" about how she had found lipstick on her husband's collar, evidence of an affair he was having. On that same record, she had a song called "You Better Go Now," which Ella Fitzgerald called her favorite of all Billie's songs.

Billie had started making good money through all her success. Between 1944 and 1947, she made $250,000 (Holiday & Dufty, 2011). She was ranked as the number one female singer by music papers all across the country and continuously sold hundreds of thousands of records. She had made it.

### *The United States vs Billie Holiday*

As I said, Billie was a woman who held multitudes. She was successful beyond her wildest dreams—she was also still very troubled. In 1947, she was arrested for the possession of narcotics in New York. Researchers believe that this arrest came as a result of her song "Strange Fruit," which had put her on a government watchlist. When Harry Anslinger, head of the Federal Bureau of Narcotics, found out that she was using heroin, he sought to use this as a way to silence the singer (Wells, 2020a).

Billie felt as though it was her versus the United States (a sentiment later echoed in the title of Lee Daniels' 2021 biographical film of Billie's life). The country was starting to ramp up its "war on drugs," and she felt as though she was a patsy for their cause.

Her treatment after the arrest was horrible. She was dehydrated and unable to eat, finally pleading guilty in return, asking to be sent to the hospital. Her request was not granted, and she was sentenced to a year and a day in federal prison (Wells, 2020a). Due to her conviction, she also lost her New York Cabaret Card, which meant that she could no longer perform at venues that sold alcohol.

She was released in 1948 on a good behavior bond.

## *Return to Music*

In the same month of her release, Billie Holiday returned to music—in a big way. She played a sold-out show at one of the world's most famous venues, Carnegie Hall. She performed all her hits, including "Strange Fruit."

In 1949, following the second arrest for drug possession in San Francisco, she recorded "Crazy He Calls Me," which was another one of her songs that was later inducted into the Grammy Hall of Fame.

By the 1950s, Billie's health was deteriorating, and so was her stamina. She was still frequently using drugs and alcohol and had several abusive relationships with men, including at least one with a drug dealer. Her ability to sing was declining as she wasn't taking care of her voice.

Nonetheless, Billie performed another two sold-out shows at Carnegie Hall in 1956. She wasn't able to play at many other venues due to the loss of her cabaret card, and she spun this into a way to gain even bigger crowds. She performed in Europe, went on late night shows, and in 1959, recorded her last songs with MGM Records, titled "Last Recording."

# BILLIE'S LEGACY

Billie influenced musicians both during her life and many decades after her. The fact that arguably the biggest musician of the 1900s, Frank Sinatra, called her his biggest influence, just shows how large her impact was. She changed the face of jazz and swing music through her improvisational style and made waves as the first African-American woman to perform alongside a white band. She didn't allow anything to stop her from seeing success. She was going to do it, no matter how hard it was for her.

Billie has won four Grammy Awards posthumously. As I mentioned, she's also been inducted into several "halls of fame," including the Grammy Hall of Fame and the National Rhythm and Blues Hall of Fame.

Her impact on the civil rights movement is also amazing. She had the foresight to use her music as a way to connect with the race issues of her time in a way that no other person had done. She used the blueprint left by Bessie Smith to connect with her audience and to let them know that their issues weren't going to go unheard.

To this day, you can turn on the radio and hear Billie Holiday's music playing through your speakers. Her lyrics are timeless, and her talent is undeniable.

Billie's life shows us that even while we struggle, we can be successful. Despite her incredibly challenging early life and teenage years, she worked hard to become a star. She wasn't going to allow anything to stand in her way. Many of us have seen great difficulties in our lives, too. It can be so hard to overcome them, and it's Billie's strength shows us that we have it in us to keep going, even when things seem impossible. I look at the things that Billie had to face in her life and remind myself that no matter what I am going through, if she could overcome her roadblocks, so can I.

# 7

## ELLA FITZGERALD (1917-1996)

### FIRST LADY OF SONG

As I mentioned in Billie's story, another big star was on the scene in the mid-20th century—the famous and renowned Ella Fitzgerald. Like Billie, Ella's name is synonymous with jazz music. She has been dubbed the "Queen of Jazz" as well as the "First Lady of Song." You can see from just those two nicknames how influential she was! She, like many of the women in this book, had a difficult upbringing, and she rose from those challenges into someone that history will never forget. Ella was beloved by critics and fans alike, receiving 13 Grammy Awards, including the Grammy Lifetime Achievement Award in 1967. She sold over 40 million albums in her lifetime and held public attention for more than half a century. Ella was able to sing in nearly any jazz style and was also an accomplished bandleader and composer in the latter half of her career (Butler, 2007). Memorabilia from her performing years is on display at both the Smithsonian Institution and the US Library of Congress.

Now, I won't rehash too many of the details of the historical context of Ella's life simply because many of them mirror Billie Holiday's. However, unlike Billie and her tragically short life, Ella lived to see the peak of the Civil Rights Movement. During this time, she became a massive activist. She met with club owners to promote equality and end segregation at the venues she was performing in. She was even arrested after one club tried to integrate their audience with little success. She specifically signed with one manager, Norman Granz, because he was also a civil rights activist. Thanks to her contribution to ending segregation, Ella was awarded the Equal Justice Award and the American Black Achievement Award by the National Association for the Advancement of Colored People (NAACP) in the 1980s (Kuske, 2016). In her lifetime, Ella saw segregation come to an end in 1964 with the passing of the Civil Rights Act. She watched as African-American people seized their rights, particularly African-American women who gained the right to vote in 1965. And she saw so much more—for Ella had a long life. She was born right before the Great Depression; she lived through the destruction of World War II, and watched as the counterculture movement spread through the United States in the 1970s. During her 79 years, she saw 15 different US presidents take office.

Ella Fitzgerald managed to remain relevant for decades. She kept up with the times, and generation after generation of music lovers got to experience her reign firsthand. Again, like all women, Ella was a complex person. Her outward personality was confident and happy to be in the spotlight. She was incredibly determined to be successful in her career and stopped at nothing to achieve her goals.

Privately, she was known for being shy and reserved. In their book *Discovering Great Singers of Classic Pop*, Roy Hemming and David Hajdu rather rudely describe her as plain-featured and rarely charismatic but that her talent shone through (Hemming & Hajdu, 1991). She was often self-conscious about the way she looked and how the public perceived her. While she was one of the most talented musicians of her era (and of all time), she even questioned her own abilities from time to time. It's a nice reminder that we are all allowed to have insecurities. Even if we are achieving success, we are allowed to doubt ourselves. It doesn't make us weak or unaccomplished—it just makes us human. We can all follow in Ella's footsteps and overcome the irksome feeling that we aren't good enough. Our doubts don't define us—our perseverance does.

# A Brief History

Ella Jane Fitzgerald was born on the 25th of April, 1917, in Newport News, Virginia. Her father, William Fitzgerald and her mother, Temperance Henry (nicknamed Tempie), were unmarried at the time of her birth. They had no other children together. Interestingly, they were both described as being "mulattos" by census data from the 1920s, meaning that they were both a mix of African and European descent. This is, of course, a highly derogatory classification and was very much of the times when Ella was born. By the time Ella was three, her parents had separated, and her mother had become romantically involved with a Portuguese immigrant by the name of Joseph da Silva. Tempie and Joseph decided to move out of Virginia and settled in Yonkers, New York, along with baby Ella. In 1923, her half-sister, Frances, was born. The two sisters were incredibly close both as they grew up and into their adulthood.

In 1925, the family moved again to a nearby area that was populated by poor Italian immigrants. The family certainly wasn't rich, and they did prioritize education. When she was six, Ella began to attend school. She reportedly was a fantastic student all through her early life. She was also interested in music and dance starting when she was young. By the third grade, she was already performing for her fellow students at lunchtime. Her family was also deeply religious and attended church regularly, which was Ella's first insight into music.

Tempie Henry fostered her daughter's interest in music. She would buy her jazz records, and Ella loved listening to Louis Armstrong and The Boswell Sisters. She loved The Boswell Sisters so much that she wanted to perform and sound just like them. Unfortunately, tragedy struck Ella's life very early on. When she was 15, her mother died in a car accident. According to Stuart Nicholson in his biography of her life, Ella was abused by her stepfather (Nicholson, 2014). After her mother's passing, she was in his care for just a year before she moved to Harlem to be taken care of by her aunt.

The trauma she experienced led her to rebel. She started to skip school and became involved with the Mafia. Her job was to be a lookout at a local Mafia-affiliated brothel. This was short-lived, as authorities caught wind of the criminal activity. Ella became a ward of the state, and she was sent to the Colored Orphan Asylum in the Bronx (Bernstein, 1996). The orphanage was filled with displaced children, and it quickly became overcrowded. This led to Ella being moved to the New York Training School for Girls in Hudson, New York (Bernstein, 1996). The experience at the reform school was horrendous. Ella suffered beatings and abuse and was quick to leave as soon as she could.

Ella was out of the reform school by age 17 with no place to go. She started making money performing on the streets of Harlem in 1934. It's important to note that this was during the Great Depression. People all over the country were struggling without money or jobs, particularly in poorer areas like Harlem. Still, despite everything she went through and the challenges of the time, she was determined to become a successful musician and took every opportunity she could to get there. In her first year out of school, Ella made her debut at an amateur night at the famous Apollo Theater. Her plan was to dance, although she quickly decided that singing would make her stand out more. She sang two songs, "Judy" and "Object of My Affection," and won first prize at the event (Moret, 1996). The winner was to perform at the theater for a week. However, the Apollo didn't give Ella that opportunity because she looked poor and disheveled (Nicholson, 2014).

This was just the start. Ella wouldn't allow one setback to determine the rest of her career. She would be a star, whether the Apollo Theater liked it or not.

## ELLA AND MUSIC

Following her amateur night performance at the Apollo Theater, Ella received the chance to perform at the Harlem Opera House in 1935. The bandleader at the venue, Chick Webb, was interested in signing a female singer for his band, the Chick Webb Orchestra, and sadly was originally put off by her appearance as well. He eventually changed his tune, though, reportedly calling her "a diamond in the rough" (Holden, 1996). Chuck agreed to offer her a test run for an upcoming performance the band had scheduled at Yale University. It wasn't an easy crowd to perform in front of. It was all-white and didn't take kindly to the African-American performers. However, Ella's talent shone through.

In short, the test went well! She was asked to join the band as they took up residency at the Savoy Ballroom in Harlem. This was when Ella started recording her music. It began with a 1936 recording of "(If You Can't Sing It) You Have to Swing It." It was a big band swing number, and Ella began to experiment with scat singing and improvisation, which was hugely impressive to both the band and the crowd.

It was around this time that her contemporary Billie Holiday joined the Count Basie Orchestra. As I said in the previous chapter on Billie, she was reportedly very jealous of Ella's success, particularly as the Chick Webb Orchestra had a permanent seat at the highly popular Savoy Ballroom. People had started to compare the two starlets, noting that Billie sang with more emotion and that Ella was more vibrant and her music was more exciting. Ella also seemed mostly unphased by Billie. She was focused on herself.

In 1938, Ella recorded a rendition of the nursery rhyme "A-Tisket, A-Tasket." This was her breakout song. It became an instant hit, with radio stations all over the country playing it for their audiences. The song went on to be one of the biggest-selling records of the 1930s (Hemming & Hajdu, 1991).

When Chuck Webb died from spinal tuberculosis in 1939, Ella was grief-stricken again. Chuck had been her mentor and shining light, and like any true star, she knew that the show must go on. Ella had already tasted fame, and the success of her 1938 recording led her to become the bandleader—the band was even named "Ella Fitzgerald and Her Famous Band" or "Ella Fitzgerald and Her Famous Orchestra." She was only 22 when this happened. It was an incredible amount of pressure for someone so young and still so inexperienced. Between 1935 and 1942, Ella and the band recorded nearly 150 songs together (Nicholson, 2014). She also had a side hustle, recording under the name "Ella Fitzgerald and Her Savoy Eight" between 1935 and 1939. She released roughly 15 tracks under this name, including "It's My Turn Now" and "You Can't Be Mine (And Someone Else's Too)." If you listen to these two tracks, you'll hear just how beautiful her voice was. The songs are set to big-band swing music, and Ella sounds otherworldly.

Despite being the star, Ella wasn't paid fairly for her performances. She was dissatisfied with how much she was receiving and started to broaden her horizons away from her band. In 1942, the band played their last show together in Philadelphia. In the same year, Ella began working with The Three Keys, and she met her manager Norman Granz. She signed with Decca Records and began singing for Jazz at the Philharmonic. The swing era was dying, and Ella knew she needed to change her style to keep up with the times. She continued to perform scat singing, and this time, with jazz music. In 1945, Ella became the youngest member of the American Society of Composers, Authors, and Publishers (Butler, 2007).

By 1945, she had another hit under her belt, the enchanting "Flying Home," which critics adored both  then and now. Following that, in 1947, she recorded "Oh, Lady Be Good," which cemented her status as one of the most important jazz musicians of the 1940s. While under Decca Records, she also released "Stomping at the Savoy" and "How High the Moon." She also notably wrote a hit for Billie Holiday called "You Showed Me the Way." Additionally, she worked with Louis Armstrong on several of his albums.

### Ella in Australia

A quick story I'd like to share is when Ella hit the international scene and was recruited to join a lineup consisting of Buddy Rich and Artie Shaw for a performance in Australia in 1954. This did not go so well. Ella missed the first two shows because Pan-American Airlines ordered her, her pianist, her assistant, and Norman Granz to get off the plane. The group all sued the airline for racial discrimination, and they won! Realistically, they didn't need the money from the lawsuit, although Norman and Ella were big believers in equal rights, so they weren't going to take this one lying down.

### A Brush With Marilyn

In 1955, Norman decided to start his own record label called Verve Records. Ella was loyal to her manager and left Decca Records to join him. It was under this label that Ella produced one of her most famous records, *Ella Fitzgerald Sings the Cole Porter Song Book*. Ella had grown sick of just singing bop music, and with the freedom of Norman's new label, she allowed herself to explore whatever style she wanted. She called this record "a turning point in my life" (Holden, 1996).

Norman continued his plight for equality. He often took signs down at venues that dictated where people would sit based on their race. He spoke out against the discrimination that was hurled at Ella when they traveled through the Southern States and made sure that Ella's pay was equal to that of the white musicians under his management. At a show in Dallas, Ella, Norman, and the band were arrested because Norman had attempted to integrate the show by allowing people to sit wherever they wanted, regardless of race. It is widely reported that while at the police station, the officers had the audacity to ask Ella for her autograph (Boston Herald, 2020).

In 1955, Ella became one of the first performers to take the stage at the Mocambo nightclub in Los Angeles. This booking would be huge for Ella's career— initially, the club wasn't interested in her. There are conflicting reports as to why. Some assume it was racial discrimination. Others claim that it was because Ella wasn't glamorous enough. People didn't like that she was overweight and didn't emphasize sex appeal. Whatever the case may be, Mocambo eventually changed their tune and signed Ella. Why? Well, it was all thanks to the intervention by the biggest star in Hollywood at the time—the one and only Marilyn Monroe. Marilyn had seen Ella perform and wanted to help her break into the Los Angeles scene. Ella felt incredibly grateful for Marilyn's assistance. She said, "I owe Marilyn Monroe a real debt... she personally called the owner of the Mocambo, and told him she wanted me booked immediately, and if he would do it, she would take a front table every night" (Novak & Evans, 2020).

### Continued Success

In 1956, at age 39, Ella recorded *Ella Fitzgerald Sings the Duke Ellington Song Book*. This would be Ella's most successful and critically acclaimed record, winning the Grammy Award for Best Jazz Performance, Individual at the first-ever Grammy Awards ceremony. Ella collaborated on this album with Duke Ellington himself, who appears on about half of the tracks.

Ella began to focus primarily on touring. For years, she would push herself more than any other performer, reportedly touring 40 to 45 weeks a year nationally and internationally (Holden, 1996). She was particularly fond of Denmark, where she had a brief relationship with a local. Even after they broke up, she continued to visit the country and even bought a house there.

She also kept recording. In 1960, she recorded one of her best-selling albums, *Ella in Berlin: Mack the Knife*. This album includes the title track "Mack the Knife," where Ella improvised many of the lyrics. In that same year, Norman sold Verve Records to MGM. MGM did not re-sign Ella after her contract was up in 1967. She spent several years jumping from one label to another and experimenting with new styles. Under Capitol Records, she released *Misty Blue*, which fell more into the genre of country music. She also recorded her last hit single, "Get Ready," in 1969 in the Motown style.

By the 1990s, Ella had recorded a total of 200 albums. In 1991, at age 74, she performed for the last time.

## ELLA AND THE SILVER SCREEN

If you thought that Ella was busy, wait till I tell you about her dalliances with film and television. In 1995, she played the part of Maggie Jackson, a jazz singer, in the movie *Peter Kelly's Blues*. In 1958, she played a small part in *St. Louis Blues* and appeared once more in the 1960 film *Let No Man Write My Epitaph*.

She also frequently graced television screens, prolifically appearing on *The Frank Sinatra Show*, where she would sing for both the studio audience and the people watching the show at home. She also performed on *The Ed Sullivan Show* and *The Pat Boone Chevy Showroom*.

Ella also made some money appearing in advertisements for Memorex and KFC.

## ELLA'S LEGACY

Ella leaves behind a bevy of albums that continue to be listened to by music lovers to this day. With 13 Grammy wins under her belt and numerous chart-topping hits, there is no debate about her influence and capabilities. She leaves behind songs that continue to be re-recorded by emerging artists all over the world, and her improvisation and scat singing has had a large influence on music today. She also leaves behind the legacy of being a civil rights pioneer and is remembered for her fight to see equality among the races and the sexes.

Ella was awarded the Presidential Medal of Freedom in 1992. She was commemorated on a US Postal Service stamp in 2007. Google celebrated her birthday in 2013. The world will not forget her name.

Ella is a reminder to all of us that no matter how challenging something may seem, there is always a way to achieve your goals. She wasn't a traditional star—she was often told that she didn't have the right look or right personality to make it, although it didn't deter her. In fact, it kept her going. Even the shyest and most self-conscious of women can succeed, regardless of if they doubt themselves. Ella's fight for equal rights shows grit and determination. She wasn't going to allow people to see her as "less than" just because of the color of her skin or her gender. She worked hard to prove a point. We can all do the same in our everyday lives. We have the right to speak up and leverage our talents to be heard.

# 8

---◆---

# PATSY CLINE (1932-1963)

## THE CLINE

Without Patsy Cline, there would be no Carrie Underwood or Taylor Swift. Women in country music wouldn't be where they are without this powerful and influential pioneer. As the first-ever female performer to be inducted into the Country Music Hall of Fame, she paved the way for other women to achieve the same success as her, and she is remembered as one of the most influential singers of the 20th century. She was also the first country artist to make pop music. At the time, the country music genre was dominated by men. It was seen as the music for the macho and didn't leave room for women to be successful. Patsy Cline was having none of that. With two number-one hits and millions of records sold, she proved that the genre could be dominated by women—and she made it clear that nothing was going to stop her. Patsy's life was tragically cut short when she was only 30. We can only imagine the heights she would have reached if she had had a few more decades to make an even greater mark.

Patsy Cline lived between the first and second waves of feminism in the United States. While women had the right to vote starting from 1920, things were all but equal. Women were joining the workforce during World War II in droves and thus were finally getting to be the main breadwinners of their households. However, with the men returning from war, women were once again delegated to the role of homemakers by the time the 1950s came around. The media pushed this agenda through popular television shows, and it was expected that women would project an image of perfection. Women only made up about 30% of the workforce, being employed as secretaries, teachers, and nurses. The Equal Pay Act wasn't signed until 1963. While female performers were on the rise (for example, Marilyn Monroe, Audrey Hepburn, and Ella Fitzgerald), they frequently weren't paid a fair wage in comparison to their male counterparts.

Patsy experienced this inequality. She was reportedly paid half the industry standard when she signed her first record deal, and before music, she did odd jobs that didn't pay her very well either. This may not be a fair comparison, as Johnny Cash lived much longer than Patsy, and at the time of his death, his net worth was about $60 million. Patsy's was just $10 million. June Carter Cash, who did live well into her 70s, also had an estimated net worth of $10 million. I know most of us will never see a sum so large in our lives, although I think it's a good example of inequality.

I'm going to borrow a quote from music writer Cindy Grogan, who referred to Patsy Cline as "the original badass" (Grogan, 2020). Indeed, Patsy was incredibly outspoken and independent and pushed against societal expectations of women. She drank with men (holding her own) and told crude jokes. Unlike other female singers, she dressed differently, too. When performing at the Grand Ole Opry (the Mecca of country music), she wore *pants*. In the 1960s, this was a rebellious act. Girls in schools were specifically prohibited from wearing pants, forced instead to wear dresses and skirts. Patsy's style contradicted everything people knew about female fashion.

Patsy's ability to be brash and independent in a time when society demanded demure behavior from women can spur us all on to just be ourselves. As women, we are expected to be soft creatures, and thanks to icons like Patsy, we know that we can be just as successful if we are loud and proud. Confidence is a superpower that we can all embrace. In my life, I've fallen into thinking that I should stay quiet many times if I want to be respected. Now, I demand respect by standing up for myself and being authentically me. Patsy's story is perfect for anyone struggling to find their footing and wondering how to be independent and strong.

*Note: This story contains a brief mention of sexual abuse. Reader discretion is advised.*

# A Brief History

Virginia Patterson Hensley was born on the 8th of September, 1932, in Winchester, Virginia. Her father, Samuel Hensley, was a blacksmith, and her mother, Hilda Patterson, was a homemaker. Patsy was the third of Samuel's children, with two older half-siblings who were in their teens when Patsy was born. She also had two younger siblings, John and Sylvia Mae.

Her family moved all over the state as her father desperately looked for work. The Great Depression had made it difficult to find steady employment, and Patsy was often sent to live with her mother's family. Patsy was forced to start working early to help support her family and received little formal education. She took a job plucking and cutting chickens before she was even a teenager. Patsy also had a difficult home life. Her father reportedly sexually abused her when she was young (Levin, 2020). This forced her to grow up quickly, understanding from an early age that the world could be a horrible place.

When she was 13, Patsy was hospitalized with a terrible throat infection as well as rheumatic fever. She was so sick that, at one point, her heart stopped beating. The throat infection changed how she spoke, and she referred to it as having a "booming voice" (Nassour, 2008). After several days in the hospital, Patsy returned to the world of the living and started to become interested in singing. She began performing at the local Baptist church alongside her mother, where the pair would do duets. During this time, she also taught herself piano.

By age 14, Patsy was auditioning to sing on local radio stations. She was successful, and this led to her entering talent contests that led to performances at nightclub cabaret shows.

Like many men in the Great Depression era, Patsy's father deserted his family. Patsy, who had just started attending high school at the time, was forced to drop out before finishing the ninth grade. She started working as a clerk to bring in some additional income.

Patsy had a beautiful relationship with her mother, and the two were more like sisters (Nassour, 2008). Her mother encouraged her to keep performing and singing. Patsy was quite tenacious as a teen. In 1947, at age 15, she started writing letters to the Grand Ole Opry, begging to sing at the venue. The venue managers responded, asking her to send them recordings and pictures of herself. She received the chance to audition, and she and her mother, Hilda, traveled to Nashville. They slept in the car on the way there. Unfortunately, the audition was not successful.

Not one to give up, Patsy performed in Winchester for locals, making about $10 a day for her singing. She was a smart young woman who also sold cigarettes at the club, attracting men by wearing black shorts, stockings, and a garter (Scheel, 2002). She soon became part of a group called Bill Peer and His Melody Boys & Girls. She and the bandleader, Bill, had an affair during this time that would span several years. It would even continue after she met her first husband, Gerald Cline.

In 1952, Bill Peer suggested that Patsy change her name—I suppose Virginia Hensley didn't pop enough in his opinion. She used her middle name, Patterson, and her husband's surname to become Patsy Cline.

## PATSY AND MUSIC

In 1953, now a married 21-year-old, Patsy got the chance to be a contestant on a local music show. She won and was paid $100 as a reward. She also gained a regular slot on the show *Town and Country Time* (Nassour, 2008). Once she was part of the broadcast, people started to take notice. She was praised by music writers at the time for her throaty style and singing from the soul (Nassour, 2008). She started to record demo tapes to send to record labels, and in 1954, she was signed to Four Star Records as part of a package deal that included Bill Peer as well as her husband. I can only imagine how messy this was for Patsy, given she was in a relationship with both men.

Music historians note that this was not a smart business move. She received no royalties from the records she made. Patsy had been quick to sign because she was offered $200, although it didn't breed good long-term results.

While at Four Star Records, Patsy began to experiment with a blend of gospel and country music, sometimes infused with pop. Ultimately, her time with the label was mostly unsuccessful, with most of her singles failing to become hits. She started touring, playing shows at local venues, and appearing on more television shows.

In 1955, Four Star Records allowed her to record with the much bigger and more reputable Decca Records. Her first single was recorded in Nashville, titled "A Church, a Courtroom, Then a Goodbye."

In 1957, she was invited to perform on *Arthur Godfrey's Talent Scouts*, a nationally televised program based in New York. This was her break-through. She performed the song "Walkin' After Midnight," and after receiving critical acclaim, Decca Records released the song as a single. It peaked at number two on the country and western charts and at number 12 on the pop charts. She used the money from her newfound success to pay her mother's mortgage. That same year, she released her first solo album.

At a performance back in Winchester, she met a man named Charlie Dick. Subsequently, Patsy divorced Gerald, and in 1957, she married Charlie.

Charlie was a wild man, and they fought often. They were also deeply in love, making for a rocky and exciting relationship. Patsy's strong personality and independence meant that she was a fighter, and Charlie matched her energy. After one year of marriage, Charlie was drafted for a military assignment. Patsy was pregnant at the time and gave birth to their daughter, Julie. She and her newborn moved to Tennessee permanently.

## 1961

Her career was on the rise. She signed with manager Randy Hughes, who managed to secure her bookings to perform at the Grand Ole Opry, where she was paid $50 per performance. In 1960, she achieved her dream—she became an official member of the Opry. She was still technically under contract with Four Star Records, though, and obliged to record with them. Under their management, she made "Crazy Dreams" and "Lovesick Blues." As I mentioned, when performing at the Opry,

Patsy broke with convention and didn't wear the classic gingham dress typical of female country singers. She went out there with pants and unbridled confidence.

In 1960, she officially signed with Decca Records with an advance of $1,000. The following year she recorded her smash hit "I Fall to Pieces," which reached number one on the country and western charts and, once again, number 12 on the pop charts.

The year 1961 proved to be huge for Patsy Cline. She was at the top of the charts, she gave birth to her son Randy, and just months after his birth, she was involved in a near-fatal car accident with her brother. Showing just how kind this wonderful woman was, Patsy insisted that the others involved in the accident be treated first (Whitaker, 2018). She spent a month in the hospital with a broken wrist and dislocated hip, along with a cut on her forehead (Whitaker, 2018). Three of the passengers in the car that collided with Patsy's died. Charlie rushed to the hospital to make sure he was there when she woke up.

A mere few months after the accident, Patsy was back on stage at the Opry. Wearing bright red lipstick and slacks, she thanked the audience for coming out, telling them how happy she was to be back (Wells, 2020b).

Her next single (which also was released in 1961) was the song "Crazy," written by the legendary Willie Nelson. It peaked at number two on the country charts and nine on the pop charts. Additionally, in the busiest year of her life, she released her second album *Patsy Cline Showcase*.

Just when you think I'm done talking about 1961, Patsy has another surprise for us. Later in the year, she performed at Carnegie Hall to a sold-out crowd. *Billboard Magazine* awarded her "Favorite Female Vocalist" that year. With the year still not finished, she recorded her single "She's Got You," which peaked on the country charts *again*.

### A Premonition

Several of Patsy's close friends, including June Carter Cash, recall that she had a keen sense of her own mortality—through a series of premonitions, she believed that she wouldn't live much longer (Kingsbury, 2004).

In early 1963, Patsy released her single "Leavin' on Your Mind," which topped the charts again. She laid down a few more tracks before being invited to perform at a benefit in Kansas for soldiers and sailors. The plane left Nashville and crashed in Camden, Tennessee, approximately 90 miles away. All those aboard the plane, including Patsy Cline, died instantly from the impact.

## Patsy's Legacy

Patsy was just 30 when she tragically died. In her short life, she released 102 singles and became the first ever artist to blend country with pop. Artists to this day state that she influenced their careers, including Cyndi Lauper and Kacey Musgraves. She left such an impact on the world that two mixes of her greatest hits were released posthumously and peaked on the charts.

In 1973, Patsy posthumously became the first solo female artist inducted into the Country Music Hall of Fame. In 1995, she was the recipient of the Grammy Lifetime Achievement Award. There are countless memorials commemorating Patsy's life throughout Nashville, and a museum in her honor was opened in the city in 2017.

*The Washing Post* journalist Diana Reese writes that Patsy "was what I call a pre-feminist woman. She didn't open doors; she kicked them down" (Reese, 2013).

Patsy will always be remembered for her flair and confidence. She had a stage presence like no other country musician before her and brought the genre into the realm of pop music. Over half a century after her passing, she continues to inspire women to break barriers and always keep going, no matter what.

# 9

## Aretha Franklin (1942-2018)

### Queen of Soul

There is no way that I can hear the name Aretha Franklin without immediately singing in my head, "R-E-S-P-E-C-T". With one of the most iconic songs of the 20th century under her belt, along with a total of 26 Grammy nominations (and 18 wins), Aretha is one of the biggest music powerhouses to ever exist. She's one of the world's best-selling musicians, with an estimated figure of over 75 million records sold worldwide (Wang, 2018). It's no wonder people call her the "Queen of Soul." She was an activist for African-American rights and for the rights of Native Americans, as well. Her strong stand against inequality followed her right up until her death. She stood up loud and proud for what she believed in, and she'll never be forgotten for her enormous contribution to the world.

I won't go over too much of the historical context of Aretha's life. As an African-American woman, she, too, experienced the same struggles as Billie Holiday and Ella Fitzgerald. She was born during World War II, when women were just starting to go to work, and she lived through segregation. She watched as equal rights bills were passed in her early life and saw the world evolve into a *more* equal (yet not *entirely* equal) place. Aretha was alive to watch Barack Obama, the first African-American president, take office. She even performed at his inauguration, bringing him to tears. She saw her people go from being completely marginalized by society to rising to the highest ranking in the country.

Aretha's music has taken on a life of its own. Her most famous song, "Respect," is considered to be a feminist and civil rights anthem to this day. Generation after generation has looked to her music for empowerment and guidance. Her career spanned decades, with every new cohort of music lovers becoming obsessed with her voice.

Aretha was a staunch believer in keeping her private life separate from her fame. Down to her last day, she kept quiet about her personal struggles. She was like two people in the same body. In one aspect, she was a normal woman living with everyday struggles. In another, she was an iconic diva who commanded an audience with her giant voice and alluring personality. In today's day and age, we are expected to share everything with the whole world. Social media has invited strangers into our private lives, and it can feel overwhelming. Aretha is proof that you can still be beloved while keeping your private information under lock and key. It might feel like we need to share everything all the time to remain relevant in the lives of others, although that is definitely not the case. It is up to us how much we want to share. We can still stand loud and proud about our beliefs without making our whole lives an open book. I've struggled with this dichotomy myself, and I look to Aretha for inspiration when I feel like too much is being asked of me.

## A Brief History

Aretha Louise Franklin was born on the 25th of March, 1942, in Memphis, Tennessee. Her mother, Barbara, was a pianist and vocalist. Her father, Clarence, was a Baptist minister and preacher. She grew up with a blend of music and religion in her household. Aretha's family moved a lot when she was very young, finally settling in Detroit, Michigan, when she was five years old.

Her early life was marred with instability. Her parents separated when she was six years old, and she was sent to live with her half-brother in Buffalo, New York. Her mother would visit, and she would seldom see her father during this time. When Aretha was 10, Barbara sadly passed away from a heart attack. As this was happening, her father was skyrocketing into fame in the baptist community. His sermons became renowned around the country. He was making good money and became known as the man with a "million-dollar voice" (Dobkin, 2004).

Aretha started experimenting with music right after her mother's death. She learned how to play piano by ear and dropped out of school in her sophomore year to perform. Reunited with her father, he began managing her and taking her on the road with him to perform for a wider audience. She would sing gospel hymns and was well-known in the community by the age of 12.

She was also forced into a huge responsibility at 12: She became a mother to her son Clarence, named after her father, and had a second child two years later named Edward Jordan. While Aretha was traveling and performing, her grandmother and other family members would take care of her boys. Her family was incredibly supportive of her musical aspirations and wanted to see her rise to success.

In 1956, at age 14, Aretha's father helped her sign her first record deal with J.V.B. Records, and in the same year, she recorded her first singles with the label. Her first recorded song was "Never Grow Old." That same year, she released *Songs of Faith: Aretha Gospel*, marking her first album (Manoukian, 2021).

While traveling with his daughter, Clarence Sr. became involved with prominent gospel singer Clara Ward, who was a role model for Aretha. By the time she was 16, Aretha had started to tour with civil rights leader Dr. Martin Luther King Jr. Word was spreading about this young musician. People knew that she was going to be something great.

And they were right.

## ARETHA AND MUSIC

In 1960, at age 18, Aretha wanted to make a leap into the mainstream music scene and so she moved to New York to pursue her dreams. Her father, who was still her manager, managed to get her demo records to Columbia Records, who signed her that same year. She started receiving coaching from a choreographer to help her become more of a pop singer. Her first record with Columbia was released in 1961, titled *Aretha: With The Ray Bryant Combo,* and included the song "Won't Be Long," which rose to number seven on the R&B charts. This album was a blend of jazz, rhythm and blues, and doo-wop, which was critically acclaimed. In 1962, she released two more albums with Columbia: *The Tender, the Moving, the Swinging Aretha Franklin* and *The Electrifying Aretha Franklin.*

## *First Marriage*

In 1960, Aretha also met a man 11 years her senior by the name of Ted White. They married the following year, and he started to work as her manager. This was anything but a happy marriage. Ted was a huge alcoholic known for violence. During one of Aretha's recording sessions, he got into a brawl with a member of her band. In short, he was bad news. To jump forward a little, in 1967, Aretha was supposed to be the headline act at the Atlanta Hyatt Regency, only to discover that she was banned from the hotel because, once again, Ted had gotten into a fight with someone there (Manoukian, 2021). Aretha certainly wasn't going to let a man stop her from performing, so she snuck in and still did her show anyway.

It's also speculated that Ted was abusive to Aretha. There are reports that he had "roughed her up" a few times (Manoukian, 2021). They divorced in 1970, and following that, Ted was investigated in the shooting of Charles Cooke, the brother of the famous Sam Cooke, who was also Aretha's role model.

## *R.E.S.P.E.C.T*

Back to music. Aretha was a hit. By 1964, she had already been dubbed "The Queen of Soul" after a series of successful television performances. Her songs started reaching the top 10 on the R&B charts, and she was reportedly making $100,000 per year from all her shows being smash hits. Despite being a television and concert hit, her commercial success started to wane. Columbia was not impressed that she wasn't making them more money, and in 1966, when her contract expired, she actually owed them money because her record sales weren't what they thought they would be (DeCurtis et al., 1992).

They didn't re-sign her, and in 1966, she teamed up with Atlantic Records. During her first recording session with the label, Ted got into that fight with a band member I mentioned earlier. Aretha retreated from public life after that, reportedly "disappearing" for a month, before reemerging in New York to finish the record (Manoukian, 2021).

Aretha had a couple more successful tracks, including "I Never Loved a Man (The Way I Love You)" and "Do Right Woman, Do Right Man," although her biggest hit was yet to come. It was 1967 when Aretha recorded a rendition of Otis Redding's song "Respect." The song came at just the right time. That year, there was a huge amount of social unrest, with protests against racial inequality taking place all over the country. It became a song of hope and resilience. It reached number one on the pop and R&B charts, and in 1968 the song won the Grammy for "Best Rhythm and Blues Solo Vocal Performance, Female" as well as "Best Rhythm and Blues Recording" (Manoukian, 2021).

I'm sure you know the lyrics already. Aretha was staunch about receiving payment for her performances. She insisted on being paid in cash prior to taking to the stage. She knew that many African-American artists were being ripped off, and she wasn't going to stand for that kind of behavior. She also ensured that every member of her band and backing singers were paid ahead of time. Anybody who worked with Aretha would always get what was owed to them.

Aretha also recorded two more top-ten songs, the famous "(You Make Me Feel Like) A Natural Woman" and "Baby I Love You." She suddenly had a hit-studded repertoire under her belt.

In addition to "Respect" becoming an anthem in the fight for civil rights, "(You Make Me Feel Like) A Natural Woman" was iconic for being a little nod toward embracing female sexuality and desire. It wasn't as overt as the songs by Chriss Amphlett that would come in the latter half of the century (more on that later), although it was a beautiful love song that explored sexual chemistry and a craving for connection. This was a huge breakthrough because women who looked like Aretha weren't sexualized or viewed as sex bombs like some of the other artists of the time. She made it known that all women are allowed to experience love and desire, no matter what they look like. It was a step toward body positivity and liberation for women who didn't fit societal ideals.

## *Making History*

Following "Respect," Aretha was deemed the "most successful singer in the nation" (DeCurtis et al., 1992). She continued to record, making yet another legendary track, "I Say a Little Prayer." She began to tour outside of the United States for the first time in her career, playing sold-out shows across Europe.

In 1968, she became the second-ever African-American woman to be on the cover of *Time* magazine (Manoukian, 2021). While this was a big moment in her life, she resented the way *Time* portrayed her. She felt that they focused too much on her personal life and marriage and not enough on her musical prowess. As I said, Aretha was not one to share her private life with the world. She wanted to be known for her music and nothing else. In that same year, her lifelong friend, Martin Luther King Jr., was assassinated, which was a huge blow to the civil rights movement and to Aretha personally, as well. She performed at his funeral, receiving nationwide praise.

In 1970, she continued her work as an activist. She offered to pay for the release of Angela Davis for her supposed involvement in a shooting at a courthouse in California. Angela was a well-known civil rights activist, and Aretha wanted to support her in any way that she could. She said that no amount was high enough. She wanted to see Angela go free. She spoke prolifically about the rights of African-Americans and took her time in the spotlight to highlight the injustice across the country. She also supported the rights of Native Americans and other Indigenous communities around the world. Aretha's view was that all people were equal, and she couldn't stand that the Native peoples of the land were being so marginalized and forgotten.

As I mentioned, she was also a hallmark figure in the body positivity movement. She was a "plus-sized" woman who wore what she wanted and performed in a way that was outside of the norm for other women who looked like her. Known for always wearing a fur coat, Aretha used her style to be iconic. In a performance of "(You Make Me Feel Like) a Natural Woman" at the Kennedy Center, she famously slinked out of her coat and revealed a glamorous dress underneath. Aretha promoted self-respect through all her songs and sent the message that all women could be sexy. In her own way, she moved the body positivity movement forward and set a blueprint for future performers to embrace their own bodies, no matter what they looked like.

In her personal life, she married again to Glynn Turman in 1978. She had previously missed the chance to have a perfect wedding, so she threw a big party in celebration of her union. She said that she wanted this to be "the party to end all parties" (Rindner, 2021).

She continued to rise and rise. By the end of the 1970s, Aretha had won 10 Grammy awards (Manoukian, 2021). She left Atlantic Records at the end of the decade and signed with Clive Davis's Arista Records. In 1980, Aretha took to the stage at London's Royal Albert Hall to perform in front of Queen Elizabeth II. In 1981, she achieved her first-ever gold record with "Jump to It." In 1987, she won the Grammy for Best Soul Gospel Performance for her album *One Lord, One Faith, One Baptism*. She would then go on to become the first woman to be inducted into the Rock and Roll Hall of Fame (Manoukian, 2021).

In 1998, she performed at the Grammy Awards, and this performance is noted as one of the best in the show's history. She became friends with the legendary Luciano Pavarotti and would go on to perform for Pope Francis in 2015. Down to her last recordings, Aretha was a phenomenon. In 2017, she released *Brand New Me* at age 75, which peaked at number five on the classical charts.

Her last ever public performance came in that same year at Elton John's gala in support of the AIDS Foundation.

## Aretha's Personal Struggles

While she was rising and rising beyond anybody's wildest imagination, Aretha also struggled. She was diagnosed with depression in the late 1970s. Her father was robbed in a traumatic altercation in 1979, and fell into a coma soon after. He passed away five years later, tragically never waking from the coma.

She also got divorced for the second time in 1984, with her husband finding her fame too much. He felt eclipsed by his wife and couldn't stand it. There are also rumors that he repeatedly cheated on Aretha throughout their marriage.

Aretha also struggled with health issues. She was often criticized by the public for being overweight, and when she did lose a lot of weight, it led to her having heart problems. Subsequently, she was diagnosed with pancreatic cancer. After her diagnosis, she started canceling shows and eventually succumbed to the disease in 2018.

## ARETHA'S LEGACY

By the end of her life, Aretha had recorded 58 albums and had 17 singles that reached the top 10—which is more than any other female singer in pop history (Manoukian, 2021). She had 18 Grammy Awards and a dozen more nominations to her name. She has gone down in the history books as one of the most successful musicians of all time.

And, of course, a large part of Aretha's legacy is tied to her song "Respect." As I said, to this day, it is seen as a feminist and civil rights anthem and is still played on radio stations all over the world. Countless artists have covered Aretha's songs, including Jennifer Hudson and Christina Aguilera.

President Obama spoke about Aretha, saying that she was a hallmark of American history. There is no arguing against that.

Aretha is a reminder that we can all be strong, powerful women. She is an inspiration for her musical success as well as for her fight for justice. She remained true to herself and kept her struggles out of the public eye, choosing to deal with them in her own way. Aretha Franklin remains one of the biggest names in the music industry, and her legacy is everlasting.

# 10

## JANIS JOPLIN (1943-1970)
### PEARL/THE QUEEN OF PSYCHEDELIC SOUL

Janis Joplin's flame burned for only a short time. She sadly passed away at just 27. In her 27 years on Earth, she made such an impact that the world will never forget her. Janis was a misfit and disturber of the norm starting from when she was just a young girl. As she got older, she continued to rebel against society and became an icon for the disenfranchised. She rose to fame and became one of the most successful rock stars of the 1960s. She is remembered for her amazing vocals and electric stage persona. She had five hit singles and was posthumously inducted into the Rock and Roll Hall of Fame. We can only imagine how much more she would have done if she had lived for longer.

One of the biggest shifts in American culture came when Janis was rising to fame. The counterculture movement was sweeping the United States in the 1960s as young people started to speak out against the government and inequality in the world. Their stances included women's rights, the rights of people of color, and homosexual rights. People started to protest against the Vietnam War, and for the first time in history, the government had to deal with massive backlash for its military actions. The counterculture movement also led to the rise of "hippies" as people started to see the benefits of leading a more Bohemian lifestyle. Fashion started to change. No longer did men dress in suits and women in dresses—jeans became popular and were adopted by all genders. People started to wear more color and free-flowing clothes, which are now a hallmark of mid-20th century history. Additionally, young people began to experiment with drugs, particularly psychedelics. The counterculture movement was a step forward for equal rights for many groups and was a way for people to break away from cultural expectations. It was a movement that sought freedom from the norm.

People were inspired by musicians and artists during this time—particularly by the emerging Janis Joplin. She was labeled the "darling or counterculture," and "the first counterculture pinup girl" (Tine, 2020). This movement was intrinsically linked with Janis's music and persona. Everything from her fashion to her attitude was aligned with the freedom people wanted to see.

Janis Joplin was an incredibly interesting person. Though she was brash and rambunctious onstage and off, people remember her as sensitive and thoughtful. She was intelligent and articulate and could still swear like a trouper and hold her own in a room of rowdy men. Despite only living to her mid-20s, she is fondly remembered by all in the music industry for her gentle personality as well as her astounding talent.

Janis's story is a reminder that we never truly know how many days we've got left on this Earth. And that means it's never too early to start making our mark. We should all put everything into our passions and live to be our truest selves because, in the blink of an eye, it could all be gone.

## A Brief History

Janis Lyn Joplin was born on the 19th of January, 1943, in Port Arthur, Texas. Her mother, Dorothy East, was a registrar at a business college, and her father, Seth Joplin, was an engineer. Janis was the oldest of three siblings, with Laura and Michael Joplin born after her.

Janis struggled to fit in from an early age. She always felt different from her peers. She fell into a crowd of music-loving misfits, who introduced her to singers like Bessie Smith and Ma Rainey. The group of friends started performing music together, with Janis singing folk and blues at the helm of the band.

As it is for many teenagers who feel different, high school was a particularly tough time in Janis's life. She was mercilessly bullied for being overweight and having acne. She also proudly stood up for the rights of

African-American people, which led to even more taunts from her fellow students.

Janis started to hang around some local boys who introduced her to folk and blues singers like Bessie Smith, Lead Belly and Odetta. At a party one night, she sang, imitating Odetta, and she discovered something she never knew she had – a powerful voice.

She moved on to college in 1960, starting at Lamar State College of Technology, and going on to the University of Texas in Austin. Janis would be spotted around campus in her trademark Levi jeans without shoes on, carrying around her autoharp so that she could play music whenever she felt like it (Hendrickson, 1998). While at college, she started performing with the Waller Creek Boys, singing folk music on campus. In 1962, a friend at UT offered to record her singing, and she laid down the track "What Good Can Drinkin' Do."

Janis was starting to see that college life just wasn't for her. In 1963, she decided it was time for her to pursue singing and hitchhiked from Austin to San Francisco, California, with a man named Chet Helms. Once in the city, she met Jorma Kaukonen, a blues singer who would later rise to fame as well, and the pair recorded seven tracks together. These wouldn't be released until after Janis's death.

Unlike some other singers in this book, her first recordings didn't lead to a straight path toward success. Now in her early 20s, Janis started to experiment with drugs and alcohol and began using heroin and methamphetamines. She became sickly thin, and her friends convinced her to return home and take a break from the music and drug scene. When she returned to Texas, she re-enrolled at Lamar University to study anthropology and commuted to Austin to perform at local bars. Her parents also encouraged her to seek professional help, and she began sessions with a psychiatric social worker. The social worker was very concerned about Janis's plans to be a musician. He became convinced that she would relapse into drug and alcohol abuse in this industry. Janis was undeterred and, in 1965, moved back to San Francisco.

She was ready to make something of herself.

## JANIS AND MUSIC

Janis's hitchhiking buddy, Chet Helms, was responsible for her gaining traction in the San Francisco scene. He was managing Big Brother and the Holding Company, a psychedelic rock band, and recruited Janis to join in 1966. They started performing at festivals and venues across the state. Janis very quickly relapsed and started using psychedelic drugs. Some of the shows were recorded, though none of the recordings were released until decades after Janis passed away.

In mid-1966, the band signed with Mainstream Records and went to Chicago to record their first album. The label was incredibly unimpressed and sent them back home to San Fran. When Mainstream Records did release Big Brother's singles, they sold terribly. Nonetheless, they continued to perform to crowds who loved them. Their first self-titled album was released in 1967, which led to their breakthrough performance at the Monterey Pop Festival. Their performance of the song "Ball and Chain" with Janis on lead vocals was released in theaters and played on television programs throughout the United States. Their fame was starting to grow.

Janis's story intersects with Aretha Franklin's here, as she and her band also played at the Wake for Martin Luther King Jr. along with the biggest stars of the time, including Jimi Hendrix and Joni Mitchell.

The other members of Big Brother and the Holding Company began to resent Janis for her fame. She was the only one that critics and fans alike were focusing on. *Time* magazine wrote about her, saying that she was the most powerful singer in rock music, and *Vogue* called her the most staggering woman in rock (Jacobson, 1984). It was her star power that led to the band's second album, *Cheap Thrills* reaching number one on the charts and achieving certified gold status, selling over a million copies in the first month of its release (Friedman, 1992).

The band continued to tour together, although the resentment was still there. Janis played for the last time as part of Big Brother at the end of 1968.

## *All Roads Lead to Woodstock*

Famous concert promoter Bill Graham has spoken about Janis Joplin and her rise to fame, stating (Margaritoff, 2020):

She had a tremendous amount of assurance when she got it all together onstage. Offstage and privately, she seemed to be very frightened, very timid and naive about a lot of things... I don't think [she] ever knew how to handle success. I think it created problems for Janis.

Janis's last two years of life were her biggest and best. Also, her worst. In 1969, she formed the Kozmic Blues Band, which produced a blend of psychedelic and pop music in contrast to the popular trend of hard rock at the time. She was also reportedly shooting $200 worth of heroin a day (Caserta, 1975).

The Kozmic Blues Band hit the international stage. They played a show in Frankfurt, Germany, that was so packed you could barely see the band on stage. They performed at the Royal Albert Hall in London, which was a televised performance. In 1969, they released the album *Kozmic Blues* which also achieved certified gold status. Four songs reached the top five of the charts, including "To Love Somebody" and "Little Girl Blue."

Janis and her band were asked to play at the infamous Woodstock festival in 1969. They were slated for a 2 a.m. slot, and Janis spent the hours in the lead-up shooting heroin and drinking. While this is remembered as an amazing performance, with the crowd loving the band so much that they called for an encore, people noted that Janis was struggling to dance and that her voice wasn't as fierce as usual.

Video recordings of Janis's performance are still circulated today. Even if she wasn't at her best, she made the world stand still and watch her perform. One of the most famous photos to be taken at Woodstock depicts Janis sitting down in a camping chair, pouring herself a glass of *Veuve Clicquot* into a plastic cup. She's dressed in a long-sleeve tie-dye dress, with long colorful beads hanging from her neck and a pair of signature orange-pink sunglasses on her head (Hardy, 2019). It's no wonder that she was a counterculture fashion icon. She wore this same outfit on stage, performing with a big smile on her face and a swagger filled with confidence. Her drug abuse may have dampened her abilities a little, although it's the Kozmic Blues Band performance at the festival is the one that stands the test of time. To think that people stayed up all through the night to catch a glimpse of the psychedelic rock star is astounding.

In the aftermath of the festival, Janis's drug abuse led to her struggling to perform at big shows. At Madison Square Garden, she went on a rant that almost incited a riot in the crowd (Friedman, 1992). She frequently showed up too inebriated to take the stage and gave many chaotic performances. She later said that she was actually more comfortable performing in front of smaller crowds in San Francisco, usually filled with counterculture-minded people (Willett, 2008).

## *The 27 Club*

In 1970, Janis traveled to Brazil in hopes of kicking her heroin addiction. A few months later, she was back on drugs. She also formed a new band called the Full Tilt Boogie Band and began a nationwide tour with them. They played the massive Festival Express tour alongside the Grateful Dead and Buddy Guy, with Janis dressed in loose-fitting clothes with psychedelic patterns—cementing herself as a fashion icon of the time. You may recall that Janis also paid for Bessie Smith's tombstone to be erected in this year. Bessie was a huge musical influence and inspired Janis's style greatly. Janis also married drug dealer and future novelist Seth Morgan around this time.

Later in the year, the band started recording their album, *Pearl*. Janis recorded "Me and Bobby McGee" and "Move Over," the latter of which she had written herself. The song was about how men mistreated women. It includes lyrics such as "Oh yeah, make up your mind, honey. You're playing with me." She recorded the song "Mercedes Benz" in one take on the 1st of October, 1970. This song was huge in the counterculture movement. It was about how capitalism only provided the illusion of happiness and how material goods would never bring joy. This spoke directly to the heart of hippies everywhere.

She was slated to lay down the rest of her tracks over the next few days. On the 4th of October, however, Janis was found dead in her hotel room from a drug overdose.

With her passing, Janis Joplin sadly became part of the 27 Club—a pop culture phenomenon that was popularized as many musicians met their death at this age. Just 16 days before Janis's passing, Jimi Hendrix had died at the same age. The following year, Jim Morrison would also die at 27. Years later, Kurt Cobain and Amy Winehouse would also each pass away at 27.

## Janis's Legacy

Janis's album *Pearl* was released in 1971. It was the best-selling album of her career. It was number one all over the world, including in the United States, Australia, Germany, and Canada. It was certified platinum four times over. Janis would never get to see it, she was the biggest rock star in the world.

As I mentioned, she was posthumously inducted into the Rock and Roll Hall of Fame in 1995, and in 2005, she was the recipient of a Grammy Lifetime Achievement Award. Dozens of books and movies have been made about her short life, including the critically acclaimed 2015 documentary *Janis: Little Girl Blue.*

Massive pop and rock stars credit their style to Janis Joplin. Stars such as Melissa Ethridge, Stevie Nicks, Joan Jett and Alanis Morissette. Multi-platinum, best-selling musician P!NK has said that Janis was the one who inspired her to become a singer. She said that Janis was "a woman who inspired me when everyone else... didn't!" (Simpson, 2004).

Janis is a reminder that even a troubled life can lead to success. Her complicated story goes to show that women can struggle while still being at the top of their game. She inspires me to live my own life to the fullest, and to embrace opportunities that arise rather than waiting around for a better time. Seize life now, in memory of Janis.

# 11

## KAREN CARPENTER (1950-1983)
## KC

Karen Carpenter is remembered as being "one of the most iconic vocalists in pop history" (Tauriello, 2017). She had a three-octave vocal range, and her ability to harmonize was like no other. She's been ranked as one of the greatest women in rock and roll history and even has a star on the Hollywood Walk of Fame. She inspired countless women to pursue music, including some of the most successful 20th-century names like Madonna and Shania Twain. She also lived a tragically short life. Karen struggled greatly with an eating disorder and passed away at age 32. Even in death, she left a powerful legacy. She was instrumental in bringing attention to eating disorders like anorexia nervosa, which had never been discussed by the media before. Like Janis Joplin, we can only wonder what Karen could have done if she had lived a longer life.

During Karen's lifetime, there was immersible pressure on women to look a certain way. In fact, researchers have found that "The highest reported prevalence of disordered eating occurred during the 1920s and 1980s, the two periods during which the 'ideal woman' was thinnest in US history" (Howard, 2018). Magazines all over the country were pushing women to lose weight fast and conform to this unreasonable notion of the ideal body, and it caused havoc on women's health. Karen grew up just as *Playboy* magazine was coming to the fore, and the toxic notion of how women should look spread even more. They started promoting pinup models and starlets like Marilyn Monroe, and it became expected that all women would look that way. In the 1970s, stick-thin models like Twiggy were the highest paid in their industry and graced the covers of magazines all over the world. Diet culture started to rise, as did hospital admissions for eating disorders (Howard, 2018).

Karen was greatly impacted by this pressure to look perfect, and ultimately, it led to her death. I don't think a single person can blame her for thinking that she had to be thin to be popular. It was what was expected of her. It's sad to think that this is one of the main reasons that Karen is remembered, with countless articles still being written today about her eating disorder. In actuality, she was so much more than that. She was a fun-loving person who's been described as goofy in nature (Samberg, 2013). Karen was a caring friend who loved kids and shared her generosity with anybody who crossed her path. She was also a badass musician who could sing circles around any of her contemporaries and played the drums like nobody else.

Karen's story makes me think about how much I value myself and my talents. It reminds me that I'm more important than what others think of me, and I should never let societal pressures get the best of me. We are all perfect as we are. We are more than just the way that we look, and our personalities and talents are so much more important than our appearance. It's easy to forget this when the media is always telling us that a woman's worth is all about how she looks, although we can look at Karen as a reminder that there is so much more to us.

## A Brief History

Karen Anne Carpenter was born on the 2nd of March, 1950, in New Haven, Connecticut. Her father, Harold, grew up in China, the son of missionary parents. He learned English later in life and worked in the printing industry. Agnes, Karen's mother, was a homemaker. Karen had an older brother, Richard, who was three years her senior. Richard and Karen were incredibly close. They would play baseball in the streets with neighborhood kids, and even though she was often picked last because she was a girl, Karen always proved that she was just as good as the boys. It was Richard who brought music into the family home. He was a child prodigy, playing the piano by the time he was three. Karen's own foray into the music world came at the age of four, when she started tap and ballet classes.

The two siblings were also fiercely competitive. This was only made worse by their mother's reported mean streak. She heavily favored Richard, and Karen often felt like her mother didn't love her. Richard and Karen both showed an aptitude for music, although Karen was often outshone by her brother. The family moved to Los Angeles when she was 14 so that Richard could follow his musical pursuits.

To avoid going to gym class, Karen joined the school band, where she was given the glockenspiel to play. She was completely disinterested. What she liked were the drums. She begged her parents to buy her a set. Karen was tenacious and led a months-long campaign to convince her parents that she needed a drum set. She didn't back down whenever they said no. Her mother was incredibly disproving of her daughter's passion for such a masculine instrument, although that didn't deter Karen from begging and begging. She knew she wanted to play this instrument more than anything. When they finally gave in, a friend named Frankie Chavez started to give her lessons. She took to it like a duck to water. Within months, she was able to play complex songs and could switch between traditional and popular methods. She was utterly obsessed with Beatles drummer Ringo Starr, who primarily influenced her style. Ringo was also a singer—and Karen wanted to be just like him, so she started to blend the two. She didn't instantly reveal to others that she was a superb singer. She mostly focused on drumming, and singing was just her own personal side project.

Karen started an all-girl band in high school and then went on to start performing with her brother and another bassist under the name "Dick Carpenter Trio." Richard was impressed by how talented his sister was on the drums and was yet to discover her singing talent. By the time Karen was 16, the trio was signed to RCA Records and recorded with them, although the records were never released.

In 1966, Karen joined a musical collective called The Wrecking Crew, where she first showed off her amazing voice. Joe Osborn, a member of the collective, signed Karen to his small, independent label Magic Lamp Records, and he was notably not interested in signing Richard as well.

While she was navigating the music world, Karen also started experiencing her first concerns about her weight. She considered herself to be a "chubby" girl and was worried about how this would impact her future success. While still in her teenage years, Karen started to experiment with fad diets. She was an eclectic teen who collected Disney figurines and would always be dancing around. She loved playing sports, especially baseball, and was a huge fan of the New York Yankees. She was enthusiastic about life and also desperately craved attention from her mother. While she had a pretty happy childhood, something was always missing.

By 1967, the Carpenter siblings had become a duo. They had auditioned other musicians to join them after the original member of their trio left for college though they weren't able to find anybody who could keep up with them or match their distinct style. They started recording demos in Joe Osborn's garage studio and experimented with harmonizing and mixing their sound with the drum beat. They started to develop a cult following of fans who loved their live performances. The Carpenters sounded different from anybody else on the scene, which intrigued music lovers. Hard and psychedelic rock was incredibly popular at this time, although the brother-sister duo was more experimental with harmonies and different drum sounds. It made for an exciting performance that was completely unique to them.

When Karen was 19, the duo received their big break, singing with A&M Records. The Carpenters were officially on the road to success.

## KAREN AND MUSIC

Following their signing with a major label, the duo started recording. Karen would always sing from behind a drum set, just like Ringo. They both sang on several of the tracks, and Karen played bass guitar on a few as well. She was able to pick up any instrument with ease. Richard wrote most of the songs they played, and the siblings experimented with a snare and bass drum, which created their unique sound. They recorded an album titled after their Beatles' cover, *Ticket to Ride*, and this rendition of the song peaked at number 54 on the hot 100 charts.

Karen was worried about the fact that their first single was a Beatles song. She was scared about what her idol would think. However, she worried for no reason. When Paul McCartney heard the rendition, he said that Karen had "the best female voice in the world" (Fast, 2021).

The following year, in 1970, they recorded their second album, *Close to You*. This featured two of their smash hits, the first being "(They Long to Be) Close to You," which reached number one on the charts, and the second was "We've Only Just Begun," which peaked at number two. "(They Long to Be) Close to You," originally written by Burt Bacharach, remains one of the most popular songs in pop and folk music, especially thanks to the Carpenters' incredible rendition of it. The beautiful lyrics include the opening lines, "Why do birds suddenly appear every time you are near? Just like me, they long to be close to you" (Carpenters, 1970). In 1971, they won the Grammy for Best New Artist and Best Contemporary Vocal Performance by a Duo, Group or Chorus for "(They Long to Be) Close to You."

With their popularity rising, more and more people came out to see their live performances. Only there was one issue. Nobody could see the tiny Karen from behind the drums. She stood at only 5'4 tall and was completely dwarfed by the instrument. As she was the lead vocalist on the two singles, the crowds wanted to see her front and center. So, Karen had to make the decision to come out of the shadows and into the spotlight. Karen started drumming less and less and became the frontman of the duo.

In 1973, with all eyes on her, Karen started to worry about her weight even more. She hired a personal trainer and started dieting, quickly losing 20 pounds. By 1975, she weighed only 91 pounds and appeared skeletal, causing fans and media to speculate about what was wrong with her health. She maintained that she was still healthy. This was a difficult year for the Carpenters. Karen started to collapse on stage from physical and nervous exhaustion, and Richard developed an addiction to Quaaludes, which caused them to cancel shows.

Despite their struggles, the duo continued to churn out album after album. They would drop another record nearly every year between 1971 and 1978. Their 1971 album, simply titled *Carpenters*, went four times platinum and reached number two in the United States and number 12 in the United Kingdom. They won the Grammy Award for Best Pop Vocal Performance—Duo or Group that year and were nominated for

Album of the Year. Their 1972 album *A Song for You* went three times platinum. Over the course of the decade, they were nominated for 15 Grammy Awards.

However, due to their health troubles, the Carpenters stopped touring by 1978. Karen performed solo in 1980, and was joined by Ella Fitzgerald in a duet performance of a medley of songs. Beyond this, she continued to perform on television broadcasts around the country.

In 1979, Karen started to record a solo album. However, A&M Records weren't interested in releasing it. It wouldn't be released until 1996, 13 years after Karen's death.

## Karen's Personal Life

Karen had a complicated personal life which was largely entangled with her health struggles. In 1981, she married Thomas Burris, a real estate developer nine years her senior. She desperately wanted a child, although Thomas would not abide by her wishes. He already had an 18-year-old son and ended up having a vasectomy that he refused to have reversed. As I mentioned before, Karen adored children. She had visions of herself as a mother. She wanted to give up music to raise a kid and become a housewife, in complete contrast to her rock and roll lifestyle so far. She never got her wish, and their marriage ended just 14 months later. She also reportedly dated famous comedian Steve Martin, though their relationship didn't last very long.

Karen was said to be emotionally drained in the 1980s. Her friends were concerned for her mental and physical health. This included her good friend Olivia Newton-John, who expressed her worries to her friend. Karen was determined to reach physical perfection at any cost. In 1981, she started using thyroid replacement cream to increase her metabolism. This destroyed her digestive tract. By 1982, she was admitted to the hospital.

It's theorized that the reason that Karen was so focused on her weight is that she felt that this was the only thing she could control in the world. Oftentimes, her brother had made all the decisions for the Carpenters, and she felt as though she didn't have any power over what was happening to her. She was also at the mercy of record labels and concert promoters who decided whether she would or wouldn't be performing. She was a woman clearly battling with many mental health demons that were outside of her control as well, so she did the one thing that she felt gave her some power back in her life (not to mention the fact that diet culture was growing and growing, and there was an expectation placed on starlets that they had to fit in with society's definition of the perfect body if they wanted to be successful). Women like Aretha Franklin were denigrated for their appearance frequently because they were "too big," so it's no wonder that Karen didn't want to be on the receiving end of this kind of scrutiny. It didn't help her struggles that magazines started to speculate on her health and well-being while she was trying to manage her internal struggles. Having her problems out there for all the world to see was possibly one of the worst things that a person in this situation could experience. When Karen needed understanding and help, she faced criticism and speculation. It was like she couldn't win. Women were either too "fat" or too "skinny." In fact, this is still 100% happening in today's pop culture. It's no wonder that Karen's mental health was declining.

Another struggle that Karen was dealing with was that she felt an absence of motherly love throughout her life. As I mentioned, Karen felt her mother favored her brother Richard. This continued into their adulthood. Karen felt as though nothing she ever did was good enough for her mother, and she constantly tried to prove that she was just as talented as her brother. It seemed as though nothing would change her mom's mind. This was yet another thing outside of Karen's control.

Following her hospital visit, she seemed to be on the up and up. She started recording again with her brother and, in 1983, made her last public appearance at an anniversary celebration of the Grammy Awards. She and her brother discussed plans to start touring together again, sadly, this would never come to be. Just a few days after the Carpenters decided that they would hit the road, Karen was found collapsed in her childhood bedroom. Her heart was barely beating, and she was pronounced dead at a local hospital a mere few hours later.

Her death was ruled a consequence of anorexia nervosa.

## KAREN'S LEGACY

Karen left a huge mark on the history of women in music. Debbie Peterson of the Bangles said that Karen was one of her biggest influences (Tauriello, 2017). Multiple music magazines, including *Rolling Stone*, have ranked Karen as one of the best singers of all time. Her recordings have been released in four posthumous albums, all of which were wildly successful. She remains one of the most important women to grace the stage.

Despite her talent, perhaps her biggest legacy lies in her struggles. Her family started a foundation in her name, which raises money for research into eating disorders, bringing some much-needed attention to the illness. It's such a shame that she wasn't able to see her legacy live on.

Karen Carpenter was a musical force. She was a complicated woman who struggled with mental health issues and left us far too soon. She reminds us that our health is more important than how we are perceived. And her music reminds us that we can do anything we want, including becoming arguably better than Ringo Starr.

# 12

## CHRISTINE AMPHLETT (1959-2013)

### CHRISSY

Australia is known for producing some of the biggest rock bands of all time. From AC/DC to INXS to Nick Cave and the Bad Seed, Aussies have swept the world with their unique style and charisma. To this day, bands from "down under" are some of the most prominent features of the music industry. Tame Impala and Courtney Barnett are featured in every major festival lineup, and you can't turn on the radio without hearing their songs. Their success wouldn't be possible without the bands that came before them. They owe all their popularity to the blueprint set for them—and they especially owe their thanks to one of the biggest exports from the island continent—the Divinyls. Women in rock, especially, would be nothing without the Divinyls' front woman and one of the most significant female rockers of all time—Chrissy Amphlett. Chrissy is an icon and a trendsetter. She proved to the world that women can do it all. As the leader of her band, she introduced the world to another type of rock music, one where women could stand center stage and command an audience like no others. The Divinyls reached the top 10 charts across the globe and were recognized as symbols of change in the industry. The sexy and funny Chrissy Amphlett helped them rocket through the music scene with her charming personality and never say die attitude. She was magic. She is remembered as "one of the most exciting frontpersons of any gender to grace the stages of the world" and for bringing female sexuality to a "hyper-masculine" genre (Carr, 2016). Chrissy was a feminist symbol who broke barriers. Women in music wouldn't be the same without her.

In the 1970s, Australian women were rising up. They were challenging the patriarchal ideals of the nation and finding their voice. They spat in the face of gender norms that dictated women should be demure and uninterested in sex. By the end of the decade, women in the labor force rose by 6.3%, and by the mid-1980s, 50% of women were working, compared to less than 30% in the 1960s (Ting, 2017). They still had their challenges to work through. Women were still expected to marry, and there was a huge gender pay gap that meant they often had to rely on their husbands' income to make ends meet. However, Australian women certainly weren't silent about inequality. They fought for the right to have paid maternity leave and started calling out sexual harassment in the workplace. They rallied against women having to take on "female jobs" like being teachers and nurses and started entering male-dominated industries. They paved the way for future generations to see equality, and in 1996, The Workplace Relations Act was passed, which made it illegal for men to be paid more for the same work being performed by women. Australia is now a more equal place thanks to these women.

Chrissy's influence on women cannot go unnoticed. She was a leader in demonstrating that women could be more than meek housewives and brought attention to female sexuality. Without her, pop and rock stars popular today wouldn't be able to exude sexual prowess through their music and stage performances. Her number one hit, "I Touch Myself," was a feminist anthem that encouraged women to embrace sex. She truly "broke the mould" (Kiely, 2012).

Chrissy is remembered fondly as a wild child with incredible charisma and a unique personality. She was sassy, funny, and experimental with her creativity. She took life as it came and tackled any challenges that came her way with a smile on her face and a can-do attitude. Chrissy had a passion for life and for music that spurred her on toward success. She also struggled with drug and alcohol abuse. She's another example of a complex woman who had her issues and proved that dedication and hard work could get you everything you want. As Chrissy said "Divinyls was my life and nothing else mattered. I didn't go on picnics or to the movies, or to restaurants unless it was to talk about the band. I had virtually no friends outside Divinyls and the crew." (Amphlett, 2005).

Chrissy's amazing story of success proves that women can be every-thing—and do anything—they want. She didn't allow anything to stop her from being authentic and showed that women are complicated people who don't have to conform to succeed. She reminds us that we can embrace our sexuality while still being respected. I know that even in today's society, it's not seen as "proper" for women to talk about sex in the same way that men do, although we can all work together to change that. We can honor Chrissy's legacy by being loud and proud about what makes us tick and show that our sensuality is part of who we are.

## A BRIEF HISTORY

Christine Joy Amphlett was born on the 25th of October, 1959, in Geelong, Australia. Her mother, Mary, came from a well-off family, and her father, James, was a World War II Army Veteran. She had a sister, Leigh, and was often in the company of her grandparents.

The Amphlett family loved music. Chrissy's grandparents would play piano and encourage singalongs. Her great uncle was an opera singer, and her cousin Patricia, better known as Little Pattie, was a singer who rose to her own fame. Her mother, Mary, was an enthusiastic lover of performance. She dabbled in comedy, played piano, and was famous in Geelong due to her contribution to the Geelong Musical Comedy Company. Her father ran teen dances in the community. They encouraged their daughter to embrace performance, sending her to dance and drama classes from an early age. She was also involved with the Comedy Company, and it was there she learnt how to put on a show. Her father introduced her to rock music, which she immediately loved. Chrissy took on large parts of her father's personality, remembering him as someone who had a bit of an issue with rage that later influenced her musical persona (O'Grady, 2013). Her father's wartime experiences left deep emotional scars. (Amphlett, 2005).

Chrissy's first dreams of being a rock star started when she would watch the music shows on TV, the radio's top 40 shows, and her records. Her cousin Little Pattie also had a big influence on her. She was a regular on the TV show Bandstand. Chrissy followed her career closely and would always go to see her perform when she was in Geelong. To

Chrissy, "...this was proof that an Amphlett could make it." (Amphlett, 2005).

Chrissy moved to Melbourne at age 15, a stark difference from Geelong, which was a poorer, industrial area. Now, she was in the big city. She had grown up near the coast and had grown into a surfer chick, and now found herself in a metropolitan area. She started busking on the streets and gradually started singing with bands in the club circuit of Melbourne for about a year before setting off for Europe. Overseas she continued her street performing and was even arrested and jailed in Spain for illegal busking (Adams, 2013). She spent three months behind bars. One thing that Chrissy learnt in the Spanish prison "...was that I was tough, physically and mentally, and that I was self-reliant and a survivor. So long as I believed in myself, nothing could hurt me." (Amphlett, 2005). Her time in Europe was a big learning curve. She had to sing to make a living and felt that she grew up quickly as she realized how tough the real world could be.

Three years later, now entering her 20s, she returned to Melbourne and started working in the theater as her mom had. One of her performances was in the musical *Let My People Come*, which was R-rated (O'Grady, 2013). This was her first foray into experimenting with sexuality and music together. It was here that Chrissy realized her incredible work ethic; no matter what, night after night, she showed up. Even as a child, she never missed a ballet lesson in seven years.

In 1980, she moved to Sydney to pursue a music career. Here, she would be exposed to punk bands amongst many other bands. Of course, the TV show *Countdown* also played its part in Chrissy's music evolution. Deborah Harry's video of "In The Flesh," in Chrissy's words, "changed my life" (Amphlett, 2005). Here was a woman in a bathing suit, she was strong and commanding, and she was a woman fronting a band, which was a rarity back then. This was an epiphany for Chrissy; if Deborah Harry could do it, why not her?

Chrissy worked hard singing and gigging. All the while expanding her knowledge and skills. She sang in the 2CH choir, she was singing back up in *Jesus Christ Superstar* with Marcia Hines, and gigging in bands. All the while trying to be a lead singer only to be thwarted by male singers who thought they could do better. She also scored a role in the movie *Monkey Grip,* which featured Divinyl's first EP as the soundtrack.

In 1982, while on the Sydney band circuit, director Ken Cameron was present at one of their shows. He loved their sound and recruited them to record two songs for his movie *Monkey Grip.* He also gave Chrissy, Jeremy, and Mark supporting roles in the film. One of their songs from the soundtrack, "Boys in Town," reached number eight on the Australian singles charts. This, along with their other song, "Only Lonely," became part of their repertoire. Chrissy was also nominated for an Australian Film Institute award for "best supporting actress" that year. The character Chrissy played was viewed as a symbol of female sexuality and agency.

The move to Sydney was fated—without Sydney, the Divinyls would have never come to be. She first met guitarist Mark McEntee in the car park of a small music venue in Collaroy after they were introduced by Jeremy Paul, who had been in an early configuration of Air Supply. Their paths met again shortly after at the Sydney Opera House after Chrissy and Jeremy partook in a choral concert. It wasn't until they met at the old Elephant and Castle pub in Surry Hills that they spoke to each other. Then sparks flew. Not romantically, as Chrissy explains it in her book, it was "creative electricity. We were a gang of two. Here, at last, was someone who was as manic about music as me." (Amphlett, 2005). The three musicians formed a soft rock trio before recruiting keyboard player Bjarne Ohlin and drummer Richard Harvey. This newly formed band took to the Sydney pub and club scene, performing for two years in the most popular indie venues in the city. This group was the first iteration of what would become the Divinyls, and some argue the band's best lineup.

## CHRISSY AND MUSIC

In her early days of performing, Chrissy was a little shy. She used to stand at the back of the stage with the drummer, most of the time with her back to the audience. As the band manager Vince Lovegrove describes, "She was afraid to reveal herself by performing her songs with the honest emotion they demanded." (Amphlett, 2005). Vince came up with the idea that Chrissy needed a persona to help her through. She had a theatrical background, so he thought that if she felt she was playing a character, it would help her confidence. One issue was there were no other outrageous women rock singers in Australia at that time for inspiration. Chrissy knew that if she wanted to break the mold, whatever she came up with, it had to shock and scandalize. She decided she needed to be a monster.

Inspired by AC/DC frontman Angus Young, Chrissy started performing in a "schoolgirl's uniform with suspender belt and stockings" (O'Grady, 2013). This persona transformed Chrissy into one of the most electrifying performers; Divinyls were never the same again after that.

After their first taste of success, all eyes were on Chrissy. She became known as a feminist icon and badass rock chick across the country, some of those stories were true, and others were made up as a marketing ploy. She wrote songs about the struggles girls face when wanting to express their sexuality and how hard it was for young women to fit in with "bitchy friends" (O'Grady, 2013). Some were even love songs. The songs promoted self-respect and self-love. The clubs they performed at were often filled with drunk men who would "hoot and holler" at the lyrics (O'Grady, 2013). Chrissy wasn't having any of this. She would shout back at the crowd until the men went into hiding behind their girlfriends, then she would smile and go back to performing.

### Chrissy and Mark

To understand the history of the Divinyls' success, I think it's important to explain the relationship between Chrissy Amphlett and Mark McEntee. Out of all the original members of the Divinyls, Chrissy and Mark were the two that stood the test of time. At first, it was a working relationship solely based on music. They were headed for the same destiny; Chrissy sang, and Mark played blistering, eloquent guitar. They were like brother and sister, friends and collaborators in music and nothing more. Mark was married and as far as Chrissy, and as far as Chrissy was concerned, he was off limits. (Amphlett, 2005). Then things changed after 2 years into a romantic relationship. It was from here, that the relationship became more volatile. Both of them were often fueled by drugs and alcohol and fought with each other every step of the way. The two were known to get violent with each other, only to go home together later that night. Mark had insecurities that Chrissy would leave him and while Chrissy had no intention of that, it was Mark who ended up sleeping with other people, ending the relationship 12 years later.

They were both highly creative and passionate. This tumultuous relationship is seen as a catalyst for the great art they produced together, it infused passion into their music. Chrissy and Mark were the lead performers and songwriters, and were the driving force of the Divinyls. Music was the one path that they were heading in the same direction.

## *The Rise of the Divinyls*

In a move that he probably regrets, founding member Jeremy Paul left the band after their initial success in 1982. He was replaced on the bass by Rick Grossman. In 1983, the Divinyls made Australian music history. Not only was Chrissy the first woman to front an Australian rock band, they also became the first band to be directly signed to an international label (O'Grady, 2013). They skipped over the usual step of pairing with a local label first and partnered with the label Chrysalis Records from the United Kingdom. After recording the albums *Desperate* and *What a Life!*, their hits started to roll in. At age 24, Chrissy and her band released the single "Science Fiction," which peaked at number 13 on the Australian charts. The following year they released "Good Die Young," which was number 32 on the charts. One of their most famous and enduring songs, "Pleasure and Pain," came out in 1985 and reached number 11. This song was huge (and still is huge) in Australia and catapulted them into even further success.

After cementing themselves in their home country, the Divinyls embarked on their first tour of the United States. The fascinating thing about the band was that they had an extremely loyal fan base, although they didn't have much major commercial success in the beginning. Still, they were on everybody's radar.

Throughout the 1980s, the Divinyls were viewed as a hard rock band. Chrissy was often compared to Angus Young, not only because of her trademark school uniform outfit it was also because they had similar mannerisms when performing. The band continued to have incredibly successful tours around the world—although they also had their troubles. Chrissy and Mark often blew up into massive fights, and many of the band members had huge drug abuse issues. Chrissy struggled with alcoholism which she tried to fix by frequently using cocaine (O'Grady, 2013). The band drained their bank account to support their addictions, and Chrissy accumulated millions of dollars in debt (Kiely, 2012). It also didn't help that money was owed from touring, outstanding advances from MGM, legal bills and management issues.

In 1987, Rick Grossman was replaced by Clyde Bramley. They recorded their album *Temperamental* in 1988. This album was a change of pace for the band. It had more of a modern pop sound. Despite this change, Chrissy was still Chrissy. She was the first singer to avoid the traditional image of innocence and virginity and was also brash and crude. The media criticized her overtly sexual persona and some didn't like how she conducted herself in interviews. Not that any of this bothered Chrissy. She was who she was, whether people liked it or not, and to be honest there would be no Divinyls without Chrissy.

### *I Touch Myself*

In 1990, the Divinyls released a single with the mega label Virgin Records titled "I Touch Myself," which was the biggest breakthrough the band ever had. It was their first and only song to reach number one in Australia. It was massive in the US as well, reaching number four, and in the United Kingdom, it peaked at number 10. It was a song that spurred on another wave of feminism in Australia, where women started to embrace their sexuality and aided in a movement toward sexual liberation around the world. One writer recalls her experience of watching Chrissy perform this song, writing, "I was one of a gaggle of teen girls goggling the sight of her fingering the crotch-placed pocket of a sheer black dress while on stage at the State Theatre, Sydney" (Badham, 2014). She recalls that this was an erotic awakening for audiences everywhere (Badham, 2014). If you've never heard the song (have you been living under a rock?) and are wondering what was so controversial about it, here are the lyrics to the chorus: "I don't want anybody else. When I think about you, I touch myself" (The Divinyls, 1991). Saucy stuff.

In 1991, the band teamed up again with Virgin Records to release their most successful album, *diVINYLS*, with the lead single being "I Touch Myself." It was the peak of their career, reaching number five on the Australian album charts and number 15 in the US. This album also contained the song "I Ain't Gonna Eat My Heart Anymore," which reached number 19 on the Aussie charts in 1992, as well as "I'm Jealous" which peaked at number 14 in 1995. For this album, the band added another member, drummer Charley Drayton, who had played on the *Divinyls* recording sessions in 1990 and became a band member in 1993. After being together for over a decade, Mark and Chrissy split romantically in 1993. In 1994, Chrissy and Charley started dating and fell in love. In 1999, she married Charley.

### Solo Pursuits and Health Issues

The Divinyls didn't release another album until 1995, when they teamed up with Australian label BMG to record *Underworld*. Unfortunately, it wasn't a huge success and wasn't even released in the United States. The band members (except Charley) all still struggled with addiction issues. When Mark and Chrissy broke up in 1993, it was also the beginning of the end for the Divinyls. They didn't formally split up the band although they never recorded another album again.

Over the course of 16 years, the Divinyls had 17 different men come and go as band members, all for various reasons. I couldn't possibly go through all the changes the band experienced, I do think it's proof of how rickety the group was. Still, Mark and Chrissy endured and were the only two to see the band through its entire run. Despite their long history together, the former couple barely ever spoke again.

With the band over, it was time for Chrissy to go it alone. She quit drinking in 1996 at age 37 and paid back all her debt (Kiely, 2012). Even though she was busy with the Divinyls, Chrissy hadn't forgotten her roots. In 1988, she starred in the critically acclaimed musical *Blood Brother*, playing the mother of a very young Russell Crowe. Ten years later, she returned to the stage to play the role of Judy Garland in the massive musical *The Boy From Oz*. The show went on to be a hit on Broadway and returned to Australia in 2000, with Chrissy resuming her role opposite Hugh Jackman. The show was now an arena spectacular, and people from all over the country traveled to see her performance.

In 2006, the Divinyls were inducted into the Australian Recording Industry Association Hall of Fame, where Chrissy and Mark were reunited for the first time in a decade. The band announced that they'd be going back on tour together. They recorded a single, "Don't Wanna Do This" the following year and embarked on an Australian tour.

Chrissy was struggling during her performances. She started experiencing physical instability and felt unsteady. Some assumed that she was drinking again. This was not the case at all. In 2007, Chrissy appeared on Australian national television to announce that she had multiple sclerosis. She continued to tour, headlining at the Homebake Music Festival just a day after announcing her diagnosis, and onlookers noted that she was physically and emotionally frail. She was also carrying a cane.

The Divinyls announced their official split in 2009, and in 2010 Chrissy performed the band's songs with the Australian Rock Symphony. In 2011, she joined the band The Tulips to release the single "Summer Song."

In 2010, she told the public that she had also now been diagnosed with breast cancer. The following year, she went into remission. She continued to perform with her cane by her side, still as enigmatic as ever.

Sadly, in 2013, at age 53, Chrissy passed away after the cancer returned. She had found love with Charley and a peaceful home.

## Chrissy's Legacy

One music writer has said, "the legacy she left behind as the original bad girl of Australian rock 'n' roll still burns brightly. Her charisma made her unforgettable" (Kiely, 2012). There is no other woman who has made such an impact on rock music. With a brazen, sexually charged persona and an unwillingness to conform to societal expectations, Chrissy Amphlett created the blueprint for female musicians today. Artists like Lana

Del Rey and Cardi B who sing so openly about sexuality, can credit this to Chrissy. She was a feminist icon who showed women all over the world that sexual desire is nothing to be ashamed of—it should be embraced. She sang her songs that were true to her heart.

After many years of Chrissy asking for the song to be used by the Cancer Council, finally, after Chrissy's death, the Cancer Council in Australia launched a breast cancer awareness project called "I Touch Myself," encouraging women to self-screen for the disease. A recording was later released with 10 Australian women singing Chrissy's song, including Olivia Newton-John and Chrissy's cousin Little Pattie. In 2014, it peaked at number 72 on the Australian charts.

Chrissy's ability to go from a rock 'n roll lead singer to a theater performer just shows how versatile and talented she was. Her sultry voice was completely unique, and her stage presence was unlike any other female performer. She was funny and controversial. We'll never see another character quite like her. She reminds me to be authentic every day. And she can remind us all that women can be leaders. The Divinyls would have been nothing without Chrissy's leadership, and she cut through a testosterone-filled industry with passion and charisma. All of us can do the same. If we know what we want, nothing should stand in our way of getting it. The men can move aside—we got this.

# Conclusion

The lessons we can learn from these music icons are endless. They harnessed their creativity and passion to make some of the most beautiful music in the world while also paving the way for historical change and developing anthems for equal rights activists that are still relevant today. These women were boastful, sublime, and embraced what made them unique. They made sure that they would never be forgotten.

When reflecting on the inspiration these women provide, I hope that you are able to harness their power to change your own life. Think back on the story of Hildegard von Bingen, who refused to accept her role in the male-dominated Church and struck her own path. And she did that in the 11th century! Louise Farrenc stood for equal pay and showed that talent is talent; it's not based on your gender. Dame Ethel Smith spent her life fighting for women's rights and led the suffragette movement. Nellie Melba proved that criticism can spur you on and that you can overcome grief to continue pursuing your dreams. Remember the story of Bessie Smith, who created protest music at a highly tense time in history, and the example set by Billie Holiday, who didn't allow racial discrimination to stop her from being one of the most influential women in music history. In moments of uncertainty, think about Ella Fitzgerald, who battled with insecurity and still rose to the top. When you need strength, think of Patsy Cline, who spoke out against societal expectations of women and drank and swore like a sailor. Sing along to Aretha Franklin's "Respect" when you need a boost, and remember that Janis Joplin taught us that a troubled life doesn't have to stop us from being successful. Look to Karen Carpenter when you need guidance navigating mental health issues. Finally, embrace your sexuality like Chrissy Amphlett. She'd be so proud of you for doing so.

I highly recommend creating a playlist dedicated to these women as you navigate through life. Their music has helped me in every struggle and dark moment, and has reminded me that I hold multitudes within myself that make me unique and powerful. No matter how tough things get, we all have the strength within us to keep going. Women are the most resilient people in the world. And you never have to go through it alone. Musical women in history have left us with a legacy that can guide us through any struggles that come our way, and we can blast their songs and compositions as a reminder of our own power.

Whether you are struggling with issues from your past or current problems that are taking over your life, just know that you are supported. You never have to go it alone.

If you enjoyed this book, I'd appreciate it if you could leave a rating and review. I'd love to hear which woman inspired you the most and how their story has helped you navigate through life.

If you would like to continue reading about musical women, then you will enjoy my *More Musical Women Throughout History* book. There was no way to cover all the musical stories that inspired me in one book! Thank you for coming on this journey with me. Until next time!

**Paid less because she was female. Unappreciated for her talent. Meet the women who fought for music and won.**
More Musical Women Throughout History delves into the lives of musicians such as: From Maria Mozart and Clara Schumann, to "Ma" Rainiey, Mamma Cass, Helen Reddy and more!

Remember to sign up for my newsletter to keep up to date with what is going on and new releases. As a thank you, make sure you claim your bonus copy of *Badass Cowgirls and The Lady BushrangerA*n intriguing and fun look at outlaws with spirit. As my editor said "These chapters were a blast."

If you liked my book, I would be most grateful if you could help other readers by leaving an honest review on Amazon. It helps people to get an idea about the book and helps them to a decision as to whether they will like it or not, thank you.

# ACKNOWLEDGMENTS

Thank you to everyone who helped and supported me to get this book written and published.

You all know who you are: Aliyah, Michelle, Michael, Andrew and of course family and friends, both old and new.

My beloved Kitty Kids for putting up with Mum, I am sure they are sick of hearing "Almost done....."

I would also love to thank all the wonderful women musicians out there that have inspired me over the years in one way or another.

# REFERENCES

Adams, J. (2013, July 5). *Chrissy Amphlett laneway would be a perfect Melbourne tribute.* The Guardian. https://www.theguardian.com/music/australia-culture-blog/2013/jul/05/chrissy-amphlett-melbourne-laneway

Albertson, C. (2003). *Bessie.* In Google Books. Yale University Press. https://books.google.com.au/books?id=MjtZAwAAQBAJ&redir_esc=y

Amphlett, C. with Writer L. (2005). *Pleasure and Pain, My Life.* Hachette Australia.

Ashley, T. (2022, May 22). *The Wreckers review – Glyndebourne bring Smyth's rarity to vivid and passionate life.* The Guardian. https://www.theguardian.com/music/2022/may/22/the-wreckers-reviewglyndebourne-festival-ethel-smyth

Badham, V. (2014, February 11). *Australian anthems: Divinyls – I Touch Myself.* The Guardian. https://www.theguardian.com/music/australia-culture-blog/2014/feb/11/divinyls-i-touch-myself-australian-anthems

BBC Music Magazine. (2019, November 15). *The life of Hildegard von Bingen*. Classical Music. https://www.classical-music.com/features/articles/life-hildegard-von-b ingen/

Bernstein, N. (1996, June 23). *Ward of the state; the gap in Ella Fitzgerald's life*. The New York Times. https://www.nytimes.com/1996/06/23/weekinreview/ward-of-the-sta te-the-gap-in-ella-fitzgerald-s-life.html

Billie Holiday. (2019). Bio. The Official Website of Billie Holiday. htt ps://billieholiday.com/bio/

Bogdanov, V., Woodstra, C., & Erlewine, S. T. (2003). *All music guide to the blues: The definitive guide to the blues. Backbeat Books*; Berkeley, Ca.

Boston Herald. (2020, June 26). *Ella Fitzgerald doc captures life, times of American legend*. Boston Herald. https://www.bostonherald.com/2020/06/26/ella-fitzgerald-doc-captur es-life-times-of-american-legend/

Broad, L. (2020, December 2). *Without Ethel Smyth and classical music's forgotten women, we only tell half the story*. The Guardian. https://www.theguardian.com/music/2020/dec/02/ethel-smyth-classic al-music-forgotten-women-canon-composition

Butler, G. (2007, May 23). *Ella Fitzgerald (1917-1996)*. Black Past. https://www.blackpast.org/african-american-history/fitzgerald-ella-191 7-1996/

Buzacott, M. (2021, March 2). *Ethel Smyth: The wild child of Frimley Green*. ABC Classic. https://www.abc.net.au/classic/read-and-watch/music-reads/composer -ethel-smyth-the-wild-child-of-frimley-green/13207516

Carpenters. (1970). (They long to be) *Close To You.*

Carr, M. (2016, March 8). *Lessons learned from 11 of the fiercest women in rock.* Music Feeds.
https://musicfeeds.com.au/features/lessons-learned-11-fiercest-women
-rock/

Caserta, P. (1975). *Going down with Janis.* Wiley-Blackwell.

Colby, J. P. (2019, March 28). *6 things you didn't know about Saint Hildegard of Bingen.* NewsCenter.
https://www.rochester.edu/newscenter/6-things-you-didnt-know-abo
ut-saint-hildegard-of-bingen-370772/#:~:text=Hildegard%20of%20Bi
ngen%20was%20a

Copeland, C. (2021, January 26). *The truth about Frank Sinatra and Billie Holiday's relationship.* Grunge.
https://www.grunge.com/320118/the-truth-about-frank-sinatra-and
-billie-holidays-relationship/

D'Silva, B. (2022, July 21). *Ethel Smyth: An extraordinary "lost" opera composer.* Www.bbc.com.
https://www.bbc.com/culture/article/20220720-ethel-smyththe-rebel
-composer-erased-from-history

Davidson, J. (2006). *Melba, Dame Nellie (1861–1931).* Australian Dictionary of Biography; National Centre of Biography, Australian National University.
https://adb.anu.edu.au/biography/melba-dame-nellie-7551

Day, M. (2017, May 8). *Bulldykers and lady lovers: The rumors about lesbian blues singers were all true.* Medium.
https://timeline.com/lesbian-blues-harlem-secret-f3da10ec2334

DeCurtis, A. ed, Henke, J., & George-Warren, H. (1992). *The Rolling Stone illustrated history of rock & roll: The definitive history of the most important artists and their music.* In Google Books. Random House. https://books.google.com.au/booksid=ubWAht7N7zsC&q=rick+hall+coproducet+aretha+respect&pg=PA335&redir_esc=y

The Divinyls. (1991). *I Touch Myself.*

Dobkin, M. (2004). *I never loved a man the way I love you : Aretha Franklin, respect, and the making of a soul music masterpiece.* In Internet Archive. New York: St. Martin's Press. https://archive.org/details/ineverlovedmanwa0000dobk

Duchen, J. (2021, July 29). *Farrenc, Louise.* Classical Music. https://www.classical-music.com/composers/farrenc-louise/

Fast, B. (2021, October 6). *Tormented facts about Karen Carpenter, the reluctant superstar.* Factinate. https://www.factinate.com/people/facts-karen-carpenter/

Franklin, A. (1967). *Respect.*

Friedman, M. (1992). *Buried alive: the biography of Janis Joplin.* In Internet Archive. New York: Harmony Books. https://archive.org/details/buriedalivebiogr00fried

Gaston, K. B. (2017, May 21). *Blues icon Bessie Smith was the Empress of Soul.* Www.pressreader.com. https://www.pressreader.com/usa/chattanooga-times-free-press/20170521/282449938962031

George, A., Weiser, M. E., & Zepernick, J. (2013). *Women and rhetoric between the wars.* In Google Books. SIU Press. https://books.google.com.au/books?id=d-b7C_ugNzYC&redir_esc=y

Goldstein, D. (2020). *Paris: Capital of the 19th century*. Brown.edu.
https://library.brown.edu/cds/paris/Goldstein.html

Gourse, L. (1997). *The Billie Holiday companion*. Schirmer Trade Books.

Green, N. (2019, June 3). *Six of the best works by Louise Farrenc*. Classical Music.
https://www.classical-music.com/features/articles/six-best-works-louis e-farrenc/

Grogan, C. (2020, September 8). *Patsy Cline: Original bad-ass*. Www. culturesonar.com.
https://www.culturesonar.com/patsy-cline-original-bad-ass/#:~:text=P atsy%20had%20an%20outspoken%2C%20independent

Hardy, A. (2019, August 8). *Janis Joplin's Woodstock outfit was a lesson in tie dye and individuality*. COOLS.
https://cools.com/janis-joplin-woodstock-outfit-tie-dye

Hemming, R., & Hajdu, D. (1991). *Discovering great singers of classic pop: A new listener's guide to the sounds and lives of the top performers and their recordings, movies, and videos*. In Internet Archive. New York, N.Y. : Newmarket Press.
https://archive.org/details/discoveringgreat00hemmi

Hendrickson, P. (1998, May 5). *Janis Joplin: A cry cutting through time*. Www.washingtonpost.com.
https://www.washingtonpost.com/wp-srv/style/features/joplin.htm

Her Place Museum. (2010). *Victorian Honor Roll of Women*. Her Place Museum.
https://herplacemuseum.com/wp-content/uploads/2017/03/2010-H onour-Roll-Booklet-.pdf

Hix, L. (2013, July 9). *Singing the lesbian blues in 1920s Harlem*. Collectors Weekly.
https://www.collectorsweekly.com/articles/singing-the-lesbian-blues-in-1920s-harlem/

Holden, S. (1996, June 16). *Ella Fitzgerald, the voice of jazz, dies at 79.* The New York Times.
https://www.nytimes.com/1996/06/16/nyregion/ella-fitzgerald-the-voice-of-jazz-dies-at-79.html?pagewanted=all

Holiday, B. (1939). *Strange Fruit.*

Holiday, B., & Dufty, W. (2011). *Lady Sings The Blues.* Crown.

Howard, J. (2018, March 9). *The history of the "ideal" woman and where that has left us.* CNN.
https://edition.cnn.com/2018/03/07/health/body-image-history-of-beauty-explainer-intl/index.html

Hughes, K. (2014). *Gender roles in the 19th century.* The British Library.
https://www.bl.uk/romantics-and-victorians/articles/gender-roles-in-the-19th-century

Jacobson, L. (1984). *Hollywood heartbreak: The tragic and mysterious deaths of Hollywood's most remarkable legends.* Simon & Schuster.

Johnson, A. E. (2019, November 18). *Hildegard of Bingen.* PS Audio.
https://www.psaudio.com/copper/article/hildegard-of-bingen/

Kiely, L. (2012, September 24). *Chrissy Amphlett: The original bad girl of Australian rock "n" roll.* Megaphoneoz.com.
https://megaphoneoz.com/chrissy-amphlett-the-original-bad-girl-of-australian-rock-n-roll/

Kingsbury, P. (2004). *The encyclopedia of country music*: The ultimate guide to the music. Oxford University Press.

Kitsock, G. (2014, February 11). *Hops: The beer ingredient (most) drinkers love*. Washington Post. https://www.washingtonpost.com/lifestyle/food/hops-the-beer-ingred ient-most-drinkers-love/2014/02/10/fd5daab0-8f57-11e3-84e1-27626 c5ef5fb_story.html

Klein, H. (1931). *Melba: An appreciation*. The Musical Times, 72(1058), 305–308. https://www.jstor.org/stable/916449

Kuske, R. (2016, August 19). *Ella Fitzgerald: Breaking down racial barriers with her voice*. National Museum of American History. https://americanhistory.si.edu/blog/ella-fitzgerald-voice

Levin, A. (2020, April 8). *Review: Loretta Lynn recalls friendship with Patsy Cline*. TownAndCountryToday.com. https://www.townandcountrytoday.com/lifestyle-news/review-loretta -lynn-recalls-friendship-with-patsy-cline-2238579#:~:text=Cline%20w as%20sexually%20abused%20by

Library of Congress. (2021). *Race relations in the 1930s and 1940s | Great Depression and World War II, 1929-1945*. Library of Congress, Washington, D.C. 20540 USA. https://www.loc.gov/classroom-materials/united-states-history-primar y-source-timeline/great-depression-and-world-war-ii-1929-1945/race-r elations-in-1930s-and-1940s/

Mahon, M. (2019, August 5). *How Bessie Smith influenced a century of popular music*. Npr.org. https://www.npr.org/2019/08/05/747738120/how-bessie-smith-influ enced-a-century-of-popular-music

Manoukian, M. (2021, March 25). *The heartbreaking true story about Aretha Franklin*. Grunge.com. https://www.grunge.com/365909/the-heartbreaking-true-story-about -aretha-franklin/

Margaritoff, M. (2020, September 21). *Janis Joplin was on her way to superstardom — then she joined the 27 club*. All That's Interesting. https://allthatsinteresting.com/janis-joplin-death

Martin, J. (2012, May 10). *Pope declares Hildegard of Bingen a saint*. America Magazine. https://www.americamagazine.org/content/all-things/pope-declares-hi ldegard-bingen-saint

Moret, J. (1996, June 15). *Ella Fitzgerald dies at age 78*. CNN. https:/ /web.archive.org/web/20061129231320/ http://www.cnn.com/SHOWBIZ/9606/15/fitzgerald.obit/index.html

Music by Women. (2021). *Ethel Smyth*. Music by Women. https://www.musicbywomen.org/composer/ethel-smyth/

NAACP. (2021). *History of lynching in America*. Naacp.org. https://naacp.org/find-resources/history-explained/history-lynching-a merica

Nassour, E. (2008). *Honky Tonk Angel*. Chicago Review Press.

National Museum of Australia. (2012). *Women's suffrage*. Nma.gov.au. https://doi.org/https://www.nma.gov.au/defining-moments/resources /womens-suffrage

The New York Times. (1893, June 4). *A WEEK'S MUSICAL TOPICS; GOSSIP OF CONCERT HALL AND OPERA HOUSE.* Story of Leoncavallo's New Opera, "I Pag- liacci" -- The Work Produced at Covent Garden with Success -- The Music Said to be Better Elaborated Than Mascag- ni's -- What Sir Augustus Harris Has Accomplished -- Success of Little Raoul Koczalski in London -- "Jane Annie." The New York Times. https://www.nytimes.com/1893/06/04/archives/a-weeks-musical-topi cs-gossip-of-concert-hall-and-opera-house-story.html?scp=5&sq=Melb a+AND+Pagliacci&st=p

Nicholson, S. (1995). *Billie Holiday.* In Internet Archive. Northeastern University Press. https://archive.org/details/billieholiday00nich/page/n5/mode/2up

Nicholson, S. (2014). *Ella Fitzgerald.* Routledge.

Novak, K., & Evans, M. (2020, June 5). *True story behind viral claims Marilyn Monroe "helped" Ella Fitzgerald land gig.* Metro. https://metro.co.uk/2020/06/05/true-story-behind-marilyn-monroe -helping-ella-fitzgerald-land-gig-gone-viral-12812540/

O'Grady, A. (2013, April 24). *Vocal warrior who owned the stage.* The Sydney Morning Herald. https://www.smh.com.au/national/vocal-warrior-who-owned-the-stag e-20130424-2iepo.html

Partridge, K. (2021, August 23). *11 Surprising Facts About Janis Joplin.* https://www.mentalfloss.com/article/649360/janis-joplin-music-facts

Phinney, R. (2018, February 15). *Dame Ethel Smyth - first female composer to be awarded damehood.* WXXI Classical. https://www.wxxiclassical.org/classical-music/2018-02-15/dame-ethel -smyth-first-female-composer-to-be-awarded-damehood

Rabaka, R. (2012). *Hip hop's amnesia: From blues and the black women's club movement to rap and the hip hop movement.* In Google Books. Lexington Books. https://books.google.com.au/books?id=8zNQkLXh9O0C&redir_esc =y Rascón, A. (2022, January 14). Bessie Smith, St. Louis Blues 1925 — short film. KUVO. https://www.kuvo.org/bessie-smith-st-louis-blues-1925-short-film/#:~: text=On%20this%20day%2C%20in%201925

Reese, D. (2013, March 5). *Crazy for Patsy Cline: Still popular 50 years after her death.* Washington Post. https://www.washingtonpost.com/blogs/she-the-people/wp/2013/03 /05/crazy-for-patsy-cline-still-popular-50-years-after-her-death/?noredi rect=on

Rindner, G. (2021, March 31). *How Aretha Franklin was impacted by her husbands.* Oprah Daily. https://www.oprahdaily.com/entertainment/tv-movies/a35952730/are tha-franklin-husbands/

Ruether, R. R. (2002). *Visionary women: Three medieval mystics.* Fortress Press.

Samberg, J. (2013, February 4). *Remembering Karen Carpenter, 30 years later.* NPR.org. https://www.npr.org/2013/02/04/171080334/remembering-karen-ca rpenter-30-years-later

Scheel, E. (2002, September 1). *Before she was a star, Patsy Cline paid her dues at many local nightspots.* Washington Post. https://www.washingtonpost.com/archive/local/2002/09/01/before-s he-was-a-star-patsy-cline-paid-her-dues-at-many-local-nightspots/2dbc c40b-9e4b-4115-8cb8-4ed04ce79860/

Service, T. (2014, June 24). *Symphony guide: Louise Farrenc's Third*. The Guardian. https://www.theguardian.com/music/tomserviceblog/2014/jun/24/sy mphony-guide-louise-farrenc-third-symphony-tom-service

Sexton, P. (2022, August 8). *Piece of her heart: Janis Joplin honors blues inspiration Bessie Smith*. UDiscover Music. https://www.udiscovermusic.com/stories/janis-joplin-bessie-s mith-headstone/

Shawe-Taylor, D. (2001). *Melba, Dame Nellie*. Oxford Music Online. https://doi.org/10.1093/gmo/9781561592630.article.18311

Simkin, J. (2014). *Ethel Smyth*. Spartacus Educational. https://spartacus-educational.com/Jsmythe.htm

Simpson, D. (2004, March 22). *Pink, Birmingham NEC*. The Guardian. https://www.theguardian.com/music/2004/mar/22/popandrock1

Smith, B. (1927). *Black-Water Blues*. Columbia Records.

Spiegel, T. (2020, July 14). *Women in the French Revolution: From the salons to the streets*. Blogs.loc.gov. https://blogs.loc.gov/international-collections/2020/07/women-in-th e-french-revolution-from-the-salons-to-the-streets/

Starkey, A. (2021, August 16). *Respect: The enduring legacy of Aretha Franklin*. Faroutmagazine.co.uk. https://faroutmagazine.co.uk/the-legacy-of-aretha-franklin/

Sweet, V. (1999). *Hildegard of Bingen and the greening of medieval medicine*. Bulletin of the History of Medicine, 73(3), 381–403. https://www.jstor.org/stable/44445287

Tauriello, D. (2017, September 20). *What do you know about...Karen Carpenter?* Web.archive.org. https://web.archive.org/web/20170920092529/https://www.modern drummer.com/article/december-2013-know-karen-carpenter/

Tine, S. van. (2020, March 15). *"Freedom's just another word for nothin' left to lose": Janis Joplin, the mistaken icon of the counterculture.* Tropics of Meta. https://tropicsofmeta.com/2020/03/15/freedoms-just-another-word-f or-nothin-left-to-lose-janis-joplin-the-mistaken-icon-of-the-countercul ture/

Ting, I. (2017, March 8). *Young women in the 1970s versus today - who has it better?* The Sydney Morning Herald. https://www.smh.com.au/national/young-women-in-the-1970s-versus -today--who-has-it-better-20170307-gus6bw.html

Wainwright, R. (2021, October 16). *The one person Nellie Melba was so desperate to please.* The Sydney Morning Herald. https://www.smh.com.au/culture/books/the-one-person-nellie-melba -was-so-desperate-to-please-20211014-p58zy3.html

Wang, A. X. (2018, September 5). *Aretha Franklin's estate is worth $80 million. what happens now?* Rolling Stone; Rolling Stone. https://www.rollingstone.com/music/music-news/aretha-franklin-will -what-happens-718930/

Wellesley, M. (2018, March 18). *The life of the anchoress.* The British Library. https://www.bl.uk/medieval-literature/articles/the-life-of-the-anchores s

Wells, K. (2020a, April 13). *The tragic real-life story of Billie Holiday.* Grunge.com. https://www.grunge.com/201358/the-tragic-real-life-story-of-billie-holiday/

Wells, K. (2020b, May 13). *The tragic real-life story of Patsy Cline.* Grunge. https://www.grunge.com/208856/the-tragic-real-life-story-of-patsy-cline/

Whitaker, S. (2018, June 14). *Remember the car accident that nearly ended Patsy Cline's career?* Taste of Country. https://tasteofcountry.com/patsy-cline-car-crash/

Wilcox-Lee, N. (2014, June 5). *Dame Ethel Smyth: Composer and suffragette.* Sheroes of History. https://sheroesofhistory.wordpress.com/2014/06/05/dame-ethel-smyth-composer-suffragette/

Willett, E. (2008). *Janis Joplin: "take another little piece of my heart."* Enslow Publishers.

Wolk, D., & Browne, D. (2018, August 16). *Aretha Franklin, Queen of Soul, dead at 76.* Rollingstone.com; Rolling Stone. https://www.rollingstone.com/music/music-news/aretha-franklin-queen-of-soul-dead-at-76-119453/

# ABOUT THE AUTHOR

## CHRISTINE BENNET

Christine Bennet was originally an English and History teacher. While Christine loved to share stories and educate her students, she left teaching to focus on writing. She has always wanted to write a book about some of the topics she taught at school.

> "There are so many women in history who have either been forgotten or never highlighted for the amazing things that they achieved. I find it a fascinating area to write within."
> - Christine Bennet

When Christine is not writing, she loves to spend time in her garden and has a healthy veggie patch. Her pets are very dear to her and follow her around her home, whether she is inside or out. She of course, loves reading, whether it be non-fiction or fiction.

 facebook.com/christinebennetauthor

Made in United States
Orlando, FL
03 December 2023

39943525R00093